THE PARENT & CHILD SERIES

YOUR SCHOOL-AGE CHILD

Other Avon Books by
Lawrence Kutner, Ph.D.

PARENT & CHILD

The Parent & Child Series

PREGNANCY AND YOUR BABY'S FIRST YEAR
TODDLERS AND PRESCHOOLERS

THE PARENT & CHILD SERIES

YOUR SCHOOL-AGE CHILD

LAWRENCE KUTNER, Ph.D.

AVON BOOKS ◆ NEW YORK

AVON BOOKS
A division of
The Hearst Corporation
1350 Avenue of the Americas
New York, New York 10019

Published in hardcover by William Morrow and Company, Inc.; for information address
Permissions Department, William Morrow and Company, Inc., 1350 Avenue of the
Americas, New York, New York 10019.

The William Morrow edition contains the following Library of Congress Cataloging in
Publication Data:

Kutner, Lawrence.
  Your school-age child / Lawrence Kutner.
    p.   cm.—(the parent & child series)
  Includes index.
1. Child development.   2. Child rearing.   3. School children.   4. Home and school.
I. Title.   II. Series: Kutner, Lawrence. Parent and child series.
HQ767.9.K87   1996   95-49857
305.23'1—dc20   ·   CIP

First Avon Books Trade Printing: March 1997

AVON TRADEMARK REG. U.S. PAT. OFF. AND IN OTHER COUNTRIES, MARCA REGISTRADA, HECHO
EN U.S.A.

Printed in the U.S.A.

OPM 10 9 8 7 6 5 4 3 2 1

Acknowledgments

This is the fourth book I've written on child development—the third in this Parent & Child series. Like all authors, I owe debts of gratitude to many people who have either contributed to this book or who have helped me maintain my sanity during its year-long gestation.

My work as a child behavior columnist for *The New York Times* and *Parents* magazine has been a marvelous complement to my formal training as a psychologist. It's given me the opportunity to speak with some of the brightest people working in the areas of child development, education, and psychiatry. It's also been a tremendous amount of fun, and has contributed immeasurably to my books.

Several people deserve special recognition for their help and support:

Al Lowman and B. G. Dilworth, my literary agents, have been there from the beginning, and unwavering in their faith in my work.

Toni Sciarra, my editor at William Morrow and Company, came into this four-book project in the middle and has been very supportive.

Annie Murphy, Bill McCoy, and Kate Jackson, all of *Parents* magazine, have been delights to work with. As editors, they are a writer's dream, for they use a scalpel instead of a hatchet.

Sol and Roz Kutner, my cousins, continue to teach me much about the meaning and importance of family.

Jonathan Bloomberg, M.D., a colleague and good friend, has offered both insight and support.

Eugene V. Beresin, M.D., and Robert B. Brooks, Ph.D., both of the Department of Psychiatry at Harvard Medical School, have given me ongoing encouragement and help, and lots of great stories.

Tom Hogan, an unwavering friend for twenty-five years, has seen me through the good and bad times, and truly understands the strange and divergent ways in which my mind works.

Yvette Campanella, a friend from adolescence with whom I've recently become reunited, has helped me gain insight into my own childhood and development.

Cheryl Olson, my partner in marriage, business, and life, has been an unwavering source of love and support, even while going through the stress of her doctoral program.

Finally, our son Michael is a constant reminder of why I've chosen to do this work. Watching him grow and develop has been fascinating and immensely rewarding. He has shown me new ways of looking at the world—which is what parenthood is all about.

Contents

x   *Contents*

Introduction

Why does my child lie so much? What should I do if my child is afraid to go to school? How can I help a child who's a perfectionist? When is sibling rivalry a good thing? What should a parent do to help a gifted or talented child?

These are only a few of the questions I'm routinely asked by readers of my columns and by audiences at the speeches and workshops I give across the United States and Canada. Their content reflects a special set of stages of development, generally known as the school-age years—the time from kindergarten through the sixth grade.

In previous books I've compared child development to a symphony. The intertwining melodies and motifs of cognitive and emotional development grow increasingly complex as children reach school age. The chordal support of physical growth and social relationships brings a depth and richness unseen in earlier years.

As with a symphony, the beauty can be appreciated at many levels. Watching how the developmental themes of childhood—independence, testing limits, adapting to new environments, building relationships, to name a few—repeat and modify themselves as a child grows older can bring insight and delight to parents. The soft melodies may grow bolder and louder at times, then retreat into the background. Dissonant passages momentarily grate, and then resolve themselves within a new structure. While the pathways are seldom straight or direct, the growth is ongoing.

But one need not pick child development into its components to enjoy it. The school-age years are also a time to step back and observe the interplay between the themes of emotional, cognitive, social, and physical growth. Friendships become not just stronger, but different. Games become more complex. Sibling relationships grow more intense and competitive.

There are, unfortunately, few books that take this type of integrative approach to exploring child development, especially during the school-age years. Yet I find it a particularly appropriate and powerful way of looking at children and their behavior.

My goal in writing this book has not been to list a series of problems and provide a quick-fix solution for each. Books that attempt to do that unfortunately gloss over the contexts in which children's behaviors occur. A child who lies repeatedly or who avoids school may be sending any of several messages, each of which reflects a different underlying problem. By treating the symptoms, you run the risk of missing the more important issues that caused the behaviors.

What I try to do here and in my other writings is to help adults—especially parents—step inside children's minds and view the world as they see it, without the biases, assumptions, and expectations of adulthood. By understanding our children's perspectives in combination with their development, we are better equipped to make sense of their frustrating, annoying, and delightful behaviors.

I have combined this strategy with what I think of as a tool kit of specific techniques for handling some of the most common problems seen in school-age children. The "tools" of the tool kit are given in the boxed passages that appear in each section of each chapter. Parents can use and adapt these tools to their specific needs.

When looking at any child's behavior, it's important to see the context in which it occurs. For children this age, that context is often within or related to school, which becomes an increasingly important part of children's and parents' lives.

The origin of the word *school* will probably come as a surprise to many of today's students, and even to teachers. It derives from an ancient Greek word meaning "leisure." School was a place where ideas could be discussed when one was not working. Attending school, like leisure itself, was a privilege.

The structure of the typical American or European school is largely built on anachronisms. The nine-month calendar is a throwback to the eighteenth and nineteenth centuries, when children were still needed to work in the fields as cheap or free labor for planting, tending, and harvesting crops. The emphasis, still present in so many classrooms, on passive, unchallenging behavior while sitting quietly at neat rows of uncomfortable desks dates back to industrialization, when factories needed obedient workers for repetitive tasks. The early dismissal hours and short school days of most elementary schools—and the immense and often unfulfilled need for high-quality after-school programs—show how those schools have ignored the majority of families, in which both parents, or the only parent, works outside the home.

This is an exciting time for education, since some of these anachronisms are being challenged and changed. It's important that today's parents not assume that the types of schools should look or even feel like those they attended.

That's not to say that the structures of the past should be rejected out of hand as irrelevant. In fact, one of the things I find sadly missing from so many families is the type of informal support and information system that was more common a generation or two ago.

Today's parents tend to be more physically isolated from their extended family—the people who used to provide advice, new perspectives, and routine or emergency baby-sitting—than families used to be. Odds are, when you grew up you had aunts, uncles, or grandparents living in the same city or community. These days, because of increased mobility, those relatives are more likely to live in other parts of the country. This, combined with the likelihood that children are growing up in single-parent families or families in which both parents work outside the home, means that much of the day-to-day emotional and physical support our parents and grandparents had is no longer as readily available.

That's why it's important that, as parents, we create our own support networks of relatives, neighbors, and friends. (An example would be to set up a cooperative of three families, in which each family takes a turn caring for everyone's children one evening every three weeks.) Not only do such support networks save us money on baby-sitting, but they also serve as a ready source of information that can help us recognize which of our children's behaviors and our own frustrations are normal and predictable.

Finally, I urge you to think of your child's development as an adventure for your entire family. As with most good adventures, it's the twists and turns that provide the most excitement and the best memories.

Have fun.

I

The Transition to School

> *When they have passed their fifth birthday they should for the next two years learn simply by observation whatever they may be required to learn. Education after that may be divided into two states—from the seventh year to puberty and from puberty to the completion of twenty-one years. Thus those who divide life into periods of seven years are not far wrong, and we ought to keep to the divisions that nature makes.*
>
> —ARISTOTLE (384–322 B.C.), *Politics*

It's no coincidence that cultures around the world begin sending their children to school at approximately the same age. It doesn't matter whether that education takes place in a modern urban classroom or outside a grass hut. Such consistency is telling, for it recognizes a process that extends beyond culture and reflects the changes in children's brains as they mature.

Psychologists often refer to this stage of development as "middle childhood." That phrase, too, recognizes the progress children have made so that they are mature enough to attend school. It acknowledges that they have mastered the rudiments of life—eating, communicating, forming relationships—and are ready to move on to some of the finer points.

When children reach the age of five, school becomes the focus of their lives. The first grade has a distinctly different flavor from preschool and kindergarten. The academic agendas of the teachers are more clearly defined: Learning to read simple words. Learning to add and subtract single-digit numbers. The social goals, such as making friends and sharing, begin to take a back seat.

But if you talk to children about why they like going to school—or what they enjoy about school even if they aren't having a good time overall—their answers are likely to describe the social experience more than the academic. Friendships, sports teams, cliques, and other social groups become an increasingly important part of children's lives.

Because of this, middle childhood represents a separation of sorts from the family, or at least a significant change in the relationships between parents and children. Children develop an independent social life outside of their family that is much more complex and sophisticated than their initial forays during preschool.

This is also the first time in many families that a social institution has such a profound effect on the parent-child relationship. The experience of school permeates and interacts with the course of children's physical, social, and emotional development. It becomes a context in which we can most clearly see our children's growth during these years.

It's easy for adults to forget how the world of school looks through the eyes of a child who's just beginning school. I have few clear memories of my time in the first grade. I recall waiting in the snow for the yellow school bus to come, and feeling proud that I could ride with the "big kids."

I remember the teacher sending my best friend Paul and me to the second-grade classroom during reading period because he and I had already taught ourselves to read (much to the distress of the teacher!). This was the 1950s, before *Sesame Street,* and parents were actively discouraged from teaching their children academic skills so that they wouldn't "get too far ahead." But Paul and I were bored with a class in which the other children were learning to recognize letters. During our reading periods that year we went through all the books in the libraries of the second- and third-grade classrooms, amusing and teaching ourselves despite the school's policy.[1]

But the images that remain sharpest in my mind are the ones tinged with fear. I remember the dark corridors and echoing stairways with their metal steps. It was during the Cold War, so we had that era's civil defense drills in which we were told we could protect ourselves from a nuclear bomb by hiding under our desks or going to the basement. Even at our tender ages, few of us believed it.

Mostly I remember how large the other children seemed. Fourth graders looked huge, especially when one of them would appear at our classroom door to pick up the daily attendance slips. I felt dwarfed by the size of the building and the people who surrounded me—a feeling I did not have at home.

Looking back, I can see that this was a time of great transition for my parents as well. My position as a student gave them new roles in the community and a new set of relationships with teachers and principals. For my mother, especially, this must have been disconcerting. She had immigrated to this country from Russia as a child, and had dropped out of school to work when she was in the

---

Sometimes organized programs can be less effective than simply letting young children practice their skills in their own way and at their own pace. A few years later, when I was in the fourth grade in a different school, I was put in a special advanced reading group in which the teacher gave us complex but boring texts to read and had us work with tachistoscopes—mechanical devices that forced the words to speed by us at increasingly fast rates—in the hope of improving our skills. In short, this well-intentioned teacher did everything she could to change reading from a pleasurable experience into a frustrating and painful one.

The woman who ran the class was known as the remedial reading teacher, since her primary job involved working with children who were having trouble. I had no idea what the word "remedial" meant, but it seemed to be something special. The day I was selected for the advanced class I rushed home and proudly announced to my mother that I was being sent to a remedial reading program. She almost passed out.

ninth grade. Although she was well-read and well-spoken, dealing with teachers must have been a painful reminder of her youthful decision.

I was her surrogate in school. She saw my achievements and actions, both good and bad, as reflections of her competence as a parent. Many parents I speak with today say they have the same feelings. It shows in the depth of our feelings when our children do well or poorly in school. We sometimes experience our children's academic successes or social rejections as if they were our own, for they call up vivid memories of when we were that age and felt similar pride or stings.

PREPARING FOR THE FIRST DAY

The first day of school is laden with intense emotions for both generations. Parents see it as an important marker in their children's and their own lives. Children view it with a combination of fear and excitement that reflects their perceptions of what will happen to them.

If you watch the parent-child interactions in the schoolyard or by the bus stop on the first day of school, you'll see a day filled with rituals and superstition. The children's clothes are often slightly more formal than they will be for the rest of the semester. Their hair tends to be freshly washed and recently cut. Hugs and kisses tend to last longer, reflecting the importance of the event.

Among children entering kindergarten or the first grade, the day may be punctuated by tears. Although I have no studies to back it up, I've noticed less of this in recent years, probably because children are entering group child care several years before kindergarten. Separating from their parents for the day is already comfortable.[2]

---

[2] In fact, I'm amazed at the large number of kindergartens still lagging behind the social revolution that has resulted in so many single-parent and two-worker families. A surprisingly large number of school districts offer only half-day kinder-

Children tend to pay closer attention than normal to their parents' emotions at the start of a school year. Occasionally, when I'm giving a talk to a group of parents, one—almost always a mother—will ask me if it means there's something wrong if a child is upset and tearful when he says good-bye that first morning of school. My answer is that it's not only normal (and nothing to worry about), but that parents may unconsciously encourage such tearful and melodramatic separations.

I'll ask the mother to imagine the following scene: She's taking her young daughter to her first day at school. On the way to the door, the mother gives the girl the traditional parental speech about how this day starts a new chapter in her life, follows it with a big hug and kiss, and says how proud she is. But instead of clinging a bit and shedding a tear, the daughter responds by nonchalantly saying, "Good-bye, Mom!" and walking casually through the door without looking back. I'll then ask the mother how she feels.

Almost all respond that they feel hurt, almost crushed. As parents, we want our children to take these important transitions in stride; yet we also want them to be just a little bit upset to let us know that we're not being replaced in their hearts and minds.

Like adults, children will fantasize about what a new experience

---

gartens, claiming that five-year-olds "cannot tolerate" spending more than three hours away from their parents. These are the same children, of course, who have had little difficulty spending six to nine hours a day in child care or preschool!

My son's school, which offers a full-day prekindergarten and kindergarten, and is usually very sensitive to parents' issues, surprised me with the hesitancy with which it started the school year when he was four. On the first day, he and his classmates attended for only an hour. The next day, they started late and were dismissed before noon. On the third day, half the class stayed for lunch and were sent home at the normal time; the other half left before lunch. The fourth day was a holiday. On the fifth day, those who hadn't stayed for lunch on the third day ate at school and spent the afternoon there, while those who had stayed late two days earlier were dismissed before noon.

All of this led to much confusion and frustration on the part of parents, many of whom went to great lengths to rearrange their work schedules, especially since many of the after-school programs didn't start for a few more weeks. Unfortunately, I believe it also led to unnecessary confusion among the students as well. Their school schedules were unpredictable, and didn't settle down until the second week.

will be like before they try it. Unlike the fantasies of older children, however, new pupils' fantasies may be markedly unrealistic and even terrifying—especially if the children have had little experience spending time with other children and new adults outside their home. Will the school building have a bathroom? Will they get anything to eat? If they miss the bus home, will they have to spend the night alone at the school? Some gentle reassurance about these worrisome but frequently unasked questions can make the transition to school go much more smoothly.

Children who are starting school for the first time may have fantasies about their parents' lives during the school day as well, especially if one of their parents has, until now, cared for them full-time at home. One mother in this situation told me how her four-year-old became upset one afternoon while they were walking home after she'd met him at the bus stop. It was his first week of kindergarten, and his first experience riding the school bus. After talking to him about his day, the mother casually mentioned that she'd had lunch with a relative.

The boy couldn't believe it. He'd simply assumed that his mother had spent her day waiting patiently for him at the bus stop. This common fantasy reflects the egocentrism of children this age—they believe they are the center of the universe, or at very least, the focus of all the lives around them. It's inconceivable to some four-year-olds that their mothers could have any other interests.[3]

---

[3] School buses tend to play a tremendous symbolic role in young children's development in our culture. Riding one is a novel form of independence that shows a child how our society recognizes her maturity. They can also trigger some wonderful stories that let us know how seriously young children take their new responsibilities.

When I lived in Cambridge, Massachusetts, a friend told me this delightful story about a four-year-old girl he knew. The girl had just started kindergarten, and had received the requisite beginning-of-the-school-year lecture from her teacher on school bus safety. Later that week the girl was with her father waiting in line at their bank. There was a rather large man standing ahead of them. The man wore a pager. Suddenly it went off: "*beep . . . beep . . . beep.*" The girl quickly grabbed her father by the arm and pulled him aside, shouting, "Get out of the way! He's backing up!"

CALMING FIRST-DAY JITTERS

The first day of school feels to children and parents the way the opening night of a play feels to the actors. The best way to prepare your child is to rehearse the scenes. Most schools have formal orientation programs for new students and parents that give each group a sneak preview of the school experience. Still, there are some additional things you can do that will help:

- Visit the school a week or two before classes start. Explore the areas that are of particular interest to your child, such as the playground and where the school buses will wait. If you can get into the building, be sure to point out the bathrooms and the dining room or cafeteria.

- Have your child meet some of her classmates before the school year starts. This is especially important if you're new to the community. Arranging for a few play dates over the summer will ensure that your child sees at least one or two familiar faces in her new school. Remember that this is usually best done one-on-one with children this age. Throwing a before-school party may be overwhelming and counterproductive.

- Minimize stress at home. This is, of course, easier said than done, especially if you're going through a divorce, a move, a change of jobs, or some other important and disruptive event. There are, however, some things you can do even in those situations that will help your child feel more secure at home. Preserve as many of the child's daily rituals as you can. Don't suddenly change the time you eat dinner. Go through the same bedtime routines. Predictability at home will help make the child's new experiences at school less frightening.

- Don't inadvertently add to the pressure. Children want to please their parents. Parents want to feel involved in their child's new world of school. But pumping your child for information about school may unwittingly send the message that she isn't doing well enough. For example, don't begin your afternoon conversation with your child by asking if she met anyone she liked at school today. The child knows the answer you want to hear, and may feel like a failure if she can't honestly provide it.

- Let your child know what you expect from her at school. Children sometimes pick up inaccurate or even unreasonable notions about what is expected of them in their classes, and what will happen if they fail to meet those expectations.

When my son visited his prekindergarten classroom before his first day of school, he met his teacher and told her, with a very serious look on his young face, that he would work very hard. (Since his mother, who had gone back to school when he was a toddler, was busy finishing her doctoral dissertation, he may have assumed that his teachers would have similar expectations of him at age four.)

I watched as his teacher put her hand on his shoulder and, with solemnity that matched his, told him that his most important work at school that year would be to play. He burst into a smile. He could do that!

CHANGING SCHOOLS

For older children and their parents, the first day at a new school poses different challenges. Some may see the building's unfamiliar corridors as a treacherous labyrinth speckled with the shadows of potential failure and embarrassment. Others see going to a new school as an exciting adventure or a chance to erase an earlier reputation and start afresh.

As with the weather, the single most powerful predictor of the immediate future in academia is the immediate past. If your child had been successful and happy at his former school, he'll probably do just as well at the new one. But if your child had academic or behavior problems where he was before, you should let your child know that those difficulties won't necessarily disappear just because the building and the people are new. Still, a change in schools can make children more receptive to making changes in their behavior, because a lot of the old triggers are no longer there.

Some of these changes may not be things you want. For example, the sheer number of differences and disruptions in a young child's environment may lead him to regress emotionally and socially. He may become clingy when you're with him in new situations. He may start wetting the bed at night. Such regressions are especially likely if the change in school has been accompanied by other important changes, such as a move to a new home.

These problems are almost always temporary. They usually go away as soon as the child feels comfortable with the new things in his life. Still, it's important that you address them by focusing not on the clinging and bed-wetting, but on the underlying issues that the child is probably having difficulty expressing in words. Talk to him about how he's safe and how you won't abandon him—two of the most common fears among children whose lives are disrupted. Let him know that it's OK to feel worried in a new situation, but that you'll always be there for him.

Children who transfer to new schools during elementary school face two types of adjustments: social and academic. Most will tell you that the social changes are more disconcerting, more difficult, and more important. This becomes even more true as children grow older. Between the ages of five and seven, children are very willing to accept newcomers into their social groups and activities.

While young children are more readily accepted by their new classmates, they're also more likely to have problems academically. The problem appears to lie in the way schoolwork is structured during the first few years. At this age, the skills being taught are basic, often with a new skill dependent on the one most recently learned. In arithmetic, for example, students must be able to divide before they can understand fractions.

If the classwork at the new school is a little bit ahead of what a child had learned at her old school, she may feel overwhelmed. She may misinterpret her situation and assume that she's having trouble because she's dumb. Unless helped with tutoring and encouragement, she may develop lower expectations of herself that can impede her performance for years to come.

Older children react differently from younger ones to a change in elementary schools. By the time children are about ten years old, they begin to express their anger and frustration more directly. They are struggling with their growing need for independence and self-sufficiency. Usually they have had little or no say in the events that led to the change of schools. They feel very attached to their old social groups and may find it difficult to enter new ones quickly. Their anger about going to a new school is symbolic of their anger at losing their sense of control over their lives.

Many children this age will do things like slam doors at home and yell about unrelated things at the top of their lungs, often blaming their parents for their predicament. The drama and volume reflect the intensity of their quandary: they don't know how to deal with the new situation, and they don't know how to ask for help.

TIPS FOR TRANSFERRING SCHOOLS

Here are some suggestions for helping your child weather the transfer to a new school:

- Don't play down the importance of the change to your child. That makes it even more difficult for him to start new friendships. It's often a good idea to let your child throw a small going-away party for his friends before he moves to a new house, especially if the move is far away.

That brings a sense of closure to those relationships and acknowledges their value.

• Don't assume that switching to a new school across town is easier than moving to one across the country. The key sources of stress for most children are the disruption of their lives and having to deal with a new peer group. According to research by Dr. Frederic J. Medway, a professor of psychology at the University of South Carolina who studies the effects of mobility on families, it's often more difficult for children to transfer schools within a city or school district than to transfer to another city or district. One reason is that the families of the children who move locally may not work as hard to help their children adjust.

• If you're moving over the summer, encourage your children to participate in a summer activity at their new school, like a sports program or an enrichment class. Programs like these will give them a chance to meet some of their classmates and learn the layout of the building in a less formal situation, before the new school year starts.

• Visit the new school ahead of time with your child. Ideally, both of you should meet some of the teachers and the principal. Your child might even be able to sit in on a class—although some teachers and administrators find this too disruptive. (Even going to the lunchroom or watching a gym class can make many children feel more comfortable with the idea of attending a new school.) It's also a good idea to set up a few "play dates" with some of your child's new classmates. This one-on-one experience will help ensure that your child sees at least one friendly face when he walks into school for his first day.

• Try to avoid midyear transfers. While the evidence is mixed, changing schools midyear tends to be much harder on children, because they find it more difficult to be ac-

cepted by established social groups and to cope with differences in their old and new curricula. The only major
advantage of a midyear transfer is that teachers may
spend more time helping new students adjust, since there
are almost always fewer of them than at the beginning of
the school year.

If you have a choice, the best time to have your child
change schools is during a natural break in formal education, such as the period between elementary and junior
high school. Since these are times when children from several smaller schools are merged into a larger one, a transfer student is not as likely to feel too out of place.

• Be aggressive about ensuring that your child's old school
records are sent to the new school. These records should
include, at the very least, standardized test scores, an outline of the classes the child took most recently, the textbooks used, and any evaluations of special needs.[4] If that

---

[4] If your child is young, you may want to have the old school send school
health testing records as well. When I was in training as a clinical psychologist, I
was assigned to do intelligence testing on a boy at a kindergarten in Minneapolis.
The teacher had found that the boy had difficulty keeping up with the work, and
wondered if he might be mentally retarded. Although his tests looked normal, I
noticed that when I spoke to him he kept his head cocked to one side. When I
asked him about this, he pointed to one of his ears and said that it was his "good
one."

I checked his records and noticed that his family had moved from California
during the middle of the semester. It seems that he had left his old state *before* his
school had done routine hearing screening, but entered his school in Minneapolis
after the new school had done its screening. The teacher had simply assumed that
the boy's hearing had passed the same tests as the other students', and concluded
that the child's difficulty paying attention and following directions was due to low
intelligence.

When I told this story to a friend of mine, he smiled broadly. It seems that
when he was in the first grade, his teacher had told his parents that he was retarded.
He was even put into a special class for a while. Eventually my friend's parents had
his vision tested and discovered that he was profoundly nearsighted. When he put
on his first pair of glasses, he discovered why he was having so much more trouble
than his classmates reading what the teacher wrote on the blackboard. When my
friend told me this story, he was a full professor of psychiatry and psychology—a
far cry from his teacher's off-the-cuff diagnosis of mental retardation.

isn't done, the new teachers may have no idea where to start with your child. They may use academic material that's too difficult or too easy, either of which may compound your child's frustration.

While administrators and school secretaries may promise that they'll send the records to the new school, don't trust that they'll do so. It's not that they're malicious; rather, things pile up over the summer. It's easy for such a request to be misplaced or overlooked. Instead, ask your school administration to give you copies of the records to bring to the new school. You may also want to spend time interviewing your children's teachers about what they'd like to convey to the new school, and include notes from those interviews with the formal records.

- Allow your children time to adjust. It takes up to a year for children to settle into a new school. If your children haven't assimilated in a year, you should talk to a school counselor about what's going on. It's also a good idea to tell your children that they may not feel fully accepted and accepting for that long.

WHEN TO BEGIN ELEMENTARY SCHOOL

I received a call a few years ago from a close friend of mine who is also a clinical psychologist. Her daughter had been the youngest in her kindergarten class, having made the school district's age cutoff by less than two weeks. The girl's language skills were well above most of her classmates', and she had no trouble with the academic components of kindergarten. The child's difficulty, according to the teacher, was that her social skills were not up to par. The teacher recommended that the girl spend another year in kindergarten to give her a chance to catch up.

My friend was distraught. Did this mean her daughter was already a failure at so tender an age? How did this reflect on the mother's skills as a parent if she had an "immature" child? The girl, who was sensitive to her mother's emotions, became equally upset, leading the household into greater turmoil.

Eventually the mother decided that her daughter was best off taking another year of kindergarten, but in a different school. That way the new curriculum, which focused on the arts, wouldn't simply repeat what the girl had learned the previous year.

Although I agreed with the mother's choice, had the daughter been a few months older or another school not been available, the decision would have been much more difficult. Before parents and teachers decide whether a child should be retained in an early grade, they should factor in a host of issues besides the child's academic and social achievements, including whether "transitional" programs are available.

Attitudes and policies regarding when a child should repeat or begin a grade have swung from "social promotion"[5] a generation or two ago to mandatory entrance examinations for some first-grade classes today. These shifts are most apparent in the very early grades. The percentage of children who are retained in kindergarten rather than promoted to the first grade has jumped significantly over the past two decades.

While many teachers and principals may give the impression that they're making their recommendations in a dispassionate, scientific manner, there's much evidence to belie such claims. Studies show little consistency across states or even school districts regarding what it takes to be a successful kindergartner or first grader. In 1985–86, according to the Laboratory for Educational Research at the University of Colorado at Boulder, 4.4 percent of children in kindergartens in West Virginia were asked to repeat that grade. In neighboring Virginia, the percentage was nearly double: 8.3 per-

---

[5] It was, for a while, quite common for children to be promoted from one grade to the next despite their inability to handle the academic material. The result was children who fell farther and farther behind their classmates. Although this practice, known as "social promotion," is less common, newspapers still report stories of illiterate high school graduates who can't get jobs or who have filed lawsuits against their school districts for professional malpractice.

cent! Such large differences indicate that the two states aren't using the same criteria to make their recommendations.

One possible reason for this is that many school districts have shifted their kindergarten and first-grade curricula from ones which focus on experiental learning to ones that are more formally academic.

In the former schools, young children spend most of their time doing what, to a casual observer, may look like play. They listen to stories, paint pictures, build forts and castles out of blocks, and plant small gardens. In the latter schools, children may do some of those things, but they spend a significant part of their day memorizing word spellings and addition tables, or filling out worksheets. All too often this "academic" approach, which is intended to give children an advantage in later grades, has the opposite effect and makes children feel incompetent at school. It's a bit like trying to build a fancy house by paying a lot of attention to decorative scrollwork on the porch without building an adequate foundation. It may look pretty for a few years, but it's bound to collapse.

Studies conducted by the Laboratory for Educational Research found that schools that retained fewer children in kindergarten tended to have more flexible curricula and more realistic expectations for five-year-olds. I've always been suspicious of kindergartens that take an "academic" approach by having children do worksheets to practice arithmetic problems and memorize how words are spelled. They seem to be directing their efforts more toward the emotional needs and competitive interests of the parents than to the developmental and intellectual needs of the children.

It's important to remember that the precursor to success at mathematics is the gut-level sense of mathematical relationships that young children gain by playing with blocks and cutting out paper shapes. The precursors to success with writing are listening to stories and understanding that they have a beginning, a middle, and an end. Without those fundamentals, rote memorization of spelling and arithmetic is likely to make a child feel frustrated and instill a long-lasting dislike of the subjects.

P R O M O T E   O R   H O L D   B A C K ?

A teacher's suggestion that a child be held back in a grade can leave parents in a quandary. Should you have your child repeat the class, or should you fight the system and insist that she be promoted? Here are some suggestions, based on current research, to help you make that decision and to provide the help your child needs to make a good transition to the next grade:

- Get detailed information from the teacher who's making the recommendation. This may require considerable tact and diplomacy, since some teachers become defensive and uncooperative if they feel their professionalism is being challenged. Remember that your goal is not to prove that the teacher is wrong about your child, but to gather additional information about what the apparent problems are and how they might be corrected.

  If the teacher is recommending that your child be held back, find out how the next year will be different from the previous one. Ask for specifics. Don't accept vague general statements. Consider changing schools, if that makes sense. Remember that repeating a class is like eating a reheated dinner—it's seldom as interesting or attractive as it was the first time around.

- Don't focus solely on your child's academic performance and social skills. Remember that in the early grades especially, success at school is often more a matter of how close the match is between a child's needs and the style of a particular teacher or classroom. A child who fidgets and needs to burn off a lot of energy may be labeled as "hyperactive" if he's put into a classroom with a rigid teacher who insists that the children sit quietly and pay attention for long periods of time. Yet that same child might be considered a model student in a class taught by a teacher who allows children to take frequent breaks and gives them physical outlets for their energy and enthusiasm.

• Find out about alternative programs, such as transitional kindergartens or transitional first grades. Many school districts have developed these as an acknowledgment of how diverse children's academic and social skills can be at this time in their lives. The ages five through seven are a time of tremendous and fundamental changes. In fact, some developmental psychologists refer to this period as the "five-to-seven shift," because of the impressive amount of intellectual and social growth that occurs. A child who's lagging behind her peers at age five may zoom past them a year or two later.

All of this has led the National Association for the Education of Young Children (NAEYC) to recommend that all children who are old enough for the first grade be sent there. Current thinking is that, except in extreme cases, children will catch up with their peers within a few years if they're given some extra support in the areas in which they're weak.

• Pay attention to long-term consequences of being left back or pushed ahead. Some of these can be subtle. A tall child who is left back may have more difficulty fitting in with his new classmates than would a child who is short for his age.

Also, girls may have more difficulty than boys if they're left back. Girls reach puberty several years ahead of boys. Unfortunately, the physical changes that accompany puberty in girls, especially the weight gain and redistribution, tend to be viewed negatively by many of the girls who are going through it. For boys, however, the story is different. They tend to see the increased size, strength, and speed that are part of male puberty as significant social and athletic advantages.

That means that by the end of elementary school, a girl who is a year older than her classmates may feel that she no longer fits in with them. Her development is out of sync with her peers in a detrimental way.[6] A boy who's a year older than many of his classmates, however, is more likely to feel out of sync in a positive way.

• Get a second opinion. This will probably have to be from someone outside your child's school so that you don't get caught in the web of academic politics. A local school psychologist, either in private practice or at a local college or university, is often a good resource. He or she will not only be able to test your child, but can probably fill you in on which schools in the community will likely be the best match.

• Talk to your child. All too often we forget this important point. Ask your child whether she would like to go on to the next grade. If your child says yes, you should take that very strongly into account. Some children who aren't ready to move up the ladder will tell you so, and will feel relieved at the opportunity to have another try.

---

[6] There's another potential problem for girls who hit puberty ahead of their classmates. Some of these early-maturing girls feel so awkward about the changes in their bodies that they stop spending time with girls their own age and begin to hang around with older adolescents. While this new peer group may be a match for them in terms of pubertal development, the young girls are almost always emotionally well behind the other girls. This can put them into social and sexual situations for which they're not at all ready, and may lead to disastrous consequences.

On the other hand, research shows that early-maturing girls who manage to keep their old friends during this burst of hormones may be at a distinct advantage. They tend to be viewed by their peers as leaders.

2

Academic Issues at School

I have never let my schooling interfere with my education.
—MARK TWAIN (1835–1910)

Although adults tend to glorify schools and their noble missions, there are times when, to students, a classroom seems little more than a place where they are judged. As adults we tend to forget or repress the feelings of powerlessness and fear that so often accompany elementary education. We gloss over the indignities of being told to stand in a corner or having to ask permission to use the bathroom. Yet the emotional experience leaves permanent marks on our psyches. Many adults, myself included, still occasionally dream about being back in school and taking a test for which we are poorly if at all prepared.

When trying to help a child who is having academic trouble at school, it's important to remember those buried feelings. Although mastering the rudiments of arithmetic or grammar may appear to be coldly logical tasks, they are laden with emotion—especially if those tasks prove difficult.

We can see this most clearly among children who have learning disabilities. A neuropsychology professor of mine used to do an exercise with the parents of some of these children. His goal was to teach the parents what their children felt like as they struggled in school, and to develop more empathy for their plight. First he asked the parents to trace the outline of a five-pointed star or some other moderately complex shape while they watched their hands. It took them only a few seconds to do it well. Next he had them copy another shape while they looked through glasses that inverted or laterally reversed the image or did both. A line that felt like it was going up might look like it was going down. A line to the left might appear to the right. Suddenly what had been simple became very confusing.

The parents drew their shapes more slowly than before. This time their drawings had false starts and erasures. The professor would tell the parents that he was disappointed in them—that other people had little trouble with this simple task (not true!). The parents' response to this news was to make *more* errors. At this point the professor would start yelling at the parents, telling them that he couldn't believe they were this stupid. Why didn't they just try harder? Surely if they just applied themselves they could do the task quickly!

The more the professor yelled, of course, the more frustrated the parents became and the more mistakes they made. After only a few minutes, some parents were reduced to tears. It was a dramatic demonstration of how frustrating it can feel to have certain learning disabilities, and an object lesson in why yelling at any child experiencing difficulty at school or telling him to try harder not only doesn't work but can be counterproductive. A different approach is needed—one which integrates the child's abilities with emotional support.

DEALING WITH LEARNING DISABILITIES

Helping children who have a learning disability is as tricky as walking a tightrope. If you don't keep encouraging them to try, they may interpret their disability as a sign that they're doomed to failure. But if you simply tell them to "tough it out" and ignore their learning difficulties, they'll become even more frustrated. According to Dr. Larry B. Silver, a child and adolescent psychiatrist at Georgetown University Medical School in Washington, D.C. (who, along with one of his daughters, has a learning disability that makes it difficult for him to read), if you push these children too hard, they may worry that they're not only failing in school, but failing in your eyes as well.

Typically, parents and schools try to help learning-disabled students—that is, children whose academic performance is consistently and significantly below what various measures of their overall intelligence would predict—by imposing rigid rules and fewer choices. The increased structure is supposed to help learning-disabled children organize their thoughts and learn better.

While that idea, at first blush, would seem to make sense, recent research by Dr. Edward L. Deci and others at the University of Rochester has found that it may make things worse. Those studies found that learning-disabled children tend to do better at school when the teachers and parents don't control them as much and let them make more of their own decisions.

One reason is that children are very sensitive to the difference between being controlled and being encouraged. Encouragement recognizes that the child is fundamentally competent at a task, even if he's having trouble with it. Control implies that the adults don't think he can do the task on his own. When Dr. Deci compared groups of mothers, he found that those who had children with learning disabilities were often less consistent in their expectations of their children, were less involved in the children's chores and homework, and were more controlling—which is exactly the opposite of what those children needed.

The style of parents' involvement with their children's schoolwork is also important. For parents who did well in school, having a child with a learning disability can lead them to change the way they relate to their children. Academic success becomes disproportionately important, and may even become the main focus of their relationship. This can begin a cycle of anger and alienation on both sides, and can lead to family problems that far outweigh the academic ones.

HELPING A CHILD WITH A
LEARNING DISABILITY

The most difficult problem for children who have learning disabilities is staying excited about school. All too often, they see the classroom as a place for failure and, therefore, one to be avoided. There are several things you can do as a parent to help avoid these problems:

- Examine your own attitudes first. If you find yourself getting very angry about your child's problems at school, try to step back and figure out why. Ask yourself whether you're upset at your child or upset at yourself for having "failed" in some way because your child isn't perfect.

- Get a thorough evaluation of your child from a team of professionals who specialize in learning disabilities. While public schools are required to offer such services, there are many areas of the country where this help is difficult to come by.

  One powerful alternative approach that need not be very expensive is to contact a medical center affiliated with a medical school, or a school psychology graduate training program at a local university. Both will probably offer diagnostic clinics that charge on a sliding scale depending on your family's ability to pay.

  The result of this evaluation should be not just a diagnosis but an education plan for your child. Don't be intimidated by jargon. If there's anything a member of the team says that's unclear, get it clarified.

- Don't think of a learning disability as an inability to learn. This is a trap that some children and parents fall into, often leading the child to give up and drop out of school. Even though it takes longer, see that your child masters basic skills with numbers, shapes, and letters. Pay particular attention to reading, for a problem in this area will lead to difficulties in almost every class your child will take.

• Talk about your child's emotions as well as his performance. For example, if your child has difficulty with motor coordination, talk about how frustrating it must be when his hand doesn't do what his brain wants it to do. That lets your child know that you understand how his problem feels to him, and that you accept him in spite of it. Unless he feels accepted, he has little reason to push himself to achieve.

• Remember that your child may not learn things the same way you did. Don't force a style of studying on your child because it worked for you. If that style doesn't meet your child's needs, it's likely to lead to failure and resentment. Instead, ask your child for suggestions about what might work best. Be flexible and willing to experiment. Stay in close touch with your child's special-education teachers.

Also, instead of just focusing on what your children are having difficulty doing, pay extra attention to what your children are doing well. That encourages children to try different approaches to their schoolwork so that they can make the most of their strengths. For example, some children may need to have their textbooks read to them; others have difficulty following oral instructions, but do well reading them.

By adjusting your approaches to take advantage of your child's strengths, you can help break through some of the emotional barriers that might otherwise hold him back. If your child realizes that he's fundamentally competent, even though he might not learn the same way or

> as quickly as his friends, he'll feel much better about him-
> self both in school and at home.

MAKING THE GRADE

Not every academic difficulty has its roots in a learning disability,
of course. A poor grade on a report card can be due to anything
from overwhelming family discord to simply forgetting to study.
I've written in a previous book[1] about my grave concerns about
using report cards as the main way of evaluating a child's performance at school.

In a nutshell, research on what psychologists call the validity
and reliability of traditional grades shows them both to be discon-
certingly low. With regard to validity, teachers of the same subject
or grade appear to be paying different attention to what aspects of
a student's performance should go into a grade, so the validity
("Am I measuring what I think I'm measuring?") is poor. For example, one fourth-grade teacher may consider penmanship and
grammar to be the most important parts of a class assignment to
write a fairy tale. The teacher in the next room who gives the same
assignment might emphasize creativity, paying little attention to
how neat the paper looks.

A student who does the assignment in one class is being judged
by different criteria from one who does it next door. Getting an
"A" for the semester in one classroom may mean very different
things than getting an "A" in the other classroom.[2]

---

[1] *Parent & Child: Getting Through to Each Other* (New York: Avon Books,
1991).

[2] Occasionally you'll run across a teacher whose evaluations are *inversely* correlated with other measures. One high school English teacher I had practically failed
me because he didn't like my writing. Another student I knew was also getting poor
grades from him in a different English class. I went on to become a columnist for
The New York Times. The other student had his first novel published while he was

Studies of grade reliability ("How stable are the measures I'm using?") show it to be equally questionable. While teachers tend to be pretty consistent when asked to grade the same papers or examinations at six-month intervals (test-retest reliability), if you give the same paper or examination to several teachers to grade independently (inter-rater reliability), the marks often cover a wide range—in some studies they've ranged from "B+" to "D−."

This means that a child in early elementary school who masters some of the fundamentals of arithmetic but not others may still get a good grade in the class. That grade, however, tells neither the child nor the parents what they really need to know: where are the child's strengths and weaknesses?

The other large problem with report cards is that they're issued so infrequently. If you mostly pay attention to your child's grades at the end of the semester, you may not know about potential difficulties until several months have passed.

MAKING THE MOST OF A REPORT CARD

The questionable usefulness of grades doesn't mean you should simply ignore or gloss over your child's report card at the end of a semester. Rather, you should use it as a trigger for more frequent and insightful reviews of how your son or daughter is doing at school. Here are some suggestions:

- Talk to your child about her feelings about school, not just her grades. Instead of asking her "How did you do?" or "What did you get?," ask something like "What did you learn in that class?" Once your child reaches late elementary school, you can talk about how she might use the things she learned in her life outside of school.[3] Find

---

in college. Clearly this teacher was using unusual (and questionable) criteria for judging his students' work.

[3] I still remember the delight I felt in junior high school when I used some of the basic geometry I'd learned the previous year to figure out a real-life wood-

out how she might approach the course differently if she were to take it again. Your goal is to go beyond "how well" she did, and help her see her achievements and frustrations in a larger context.

• Talk to your child's teachers. Unfortunately, too many parents have little contact with their child's teachers—and when they do speak to each other it's often only because there's a problem. Use each marking period as a reminder to have a meeting, either in person or on the telephone, with each of your child's teachers. Don't skip over the ones in whose subjects she got a good grade. Often you can learn as much from them as from those who teach the courses in which she might be having trouble.

I mention telephone conferences because it's often very difficult to arrange to meet in person with teachers outside of the scheduled parent-teacher conferences.[4] While it's best to have at least your first meeting with a teacher face-to-face, it's usually easier to schedule interim conferences over the telephone—especially if neither of you has any major concerns about your child's work or behavior at school.

• Try to avoid rewarding your child based on grades in a report card. Remember that your child has little control over what her final grade will be. Instead, reward the behaviors that lead to success at school, such as studying and turning in homework on time. Also keep in mind that small rewards are often more effective than large rewards.

---

working problem. Until that point I had seen little connection between the things I had been studying in school and the skills I would need to survive. There had been no practical context for learning about fractions or American history. It all seemed like a series of hoops I had to jump through. What a shame that my teachers did not point out the connection between studies and real life sooner.

[4] It still astonishes me that so few elementary schools offer on-site child care during scheduled parent-teacher conferences. The one thing that all of the visitors have in common is that they have young children! If your child's school doesn't offer this, raise the issue with the principal.

I often tell parents that a reward should be the icing on the cake, not the main meal. If you promise your child a bicycle for doing well in spelling and she doesn't succeed in getting the reward, she may give up studying the subject altogether. If the reward is too large, the reward becomes the focus of your child's attention instead of the behavior you want.

A more effective approach would be to tell your child that, for example, if she studies spelling an hour a day for three days and gets a certain percentage of words right on a mock quiz you give her, you'll take her out for pizza or let her rent a special videotape. That gives her some extra incentive, but doesn't overwhelm her.

- Don't insist on perfection. That does more harm than good. In fact, I've met with children who intentionally did poorly in or even failed a course because that action gave them some much-needed control over their lives (and some much-wanted power over their domineering parents). They told me there was no point in their trying to do well, because no matter how much they achieved, their parents always wanted them to do more.

- Look for patterns to your child's grades. Remember that, for many reasons, there will be fluctuations in grades both between courses in a single marking period and within the same course over time. Don't worry about a slight drop in a single course. But if you see several grades go down, especially if they go down significantly, that's often a warning sign of problems, either in school or at home.

READING PROBLEMS

Many children are kept from doing their best in elementary school because of slightly below average skills at reading and writing. These children are not learning disabled, so they don't qualify for special classes and support services. They are simply struggling harder or less effectively than their classmates.

For example, I once lived with some friends and their ten-year-old son for a few weeks. The father was a psychologist; the mother used to run a bookstore. They both had strong interests in their child becoming a good reader. Unfortunately, the boy was having difficulties reading, and it was beginning to affect his schoolwork.

The father's response to the situation involved a combination of encouragement and benign neglect in the hope that the problem would correct itself. The mother tried to help her child by having him read aloud. Unfortunately, he sensed her anxieties when he stumbled over a word, which made him even more nervous when he tried to read. This escalated the cycle, for his nervousness caused him to make more errors, which made his mother more anxious, which made the boy even more upset.

One of the things that struck me about his reading was how, if he didn't recognize a word immediately, he would guess wildly. If he saw an unfamiliar word, like "pharmacy," he wouldn't pause to sound it out or figure out what it might be from the context. Instead, he might read it as "piglet" or "pineapple"—words that have little in common with "pharmacy" other than their first letter.

I decided to see if I could help. One evening, another friend and I sat in their living room and began taking turns reading aloud some of James Thurber's *Fables for Our Time*. These are short, funny stories that a child his age as well as an adult could appreciate. The boy quickly came over and sat down. I explained that reading aloud in the evening was a tradition in my family, and that he was welcome to join us, but that there were some rules he had to follow.

I could see him grow tense, and knew he was wondering if I would force him to read aloud just like they did in school. The first rule was simple, I said. He didn't have to get all the words right. That wasn't important. But he had to use different voices for the different characters so that the listeners would know who was speaking. Acting ability was valued more than word accuracy.

The boy began to relax. After all, this was the exact opposite of what he had grown to hate in school, where the unstated goal of reading aloud was to say each and every word correctly. I'd done this on purpose, of course. By focusing on each individual word, he was losing sight of what the whole story was about. That made it more difficult for him to figure out a word by looking at its context. But if he were to use different voices for the characters, he had to pay attention to the larger issues in the story. Besides, speaking in different voices was fun.

The second rule, I said, was that he couldn't read more than one story before passing the book to the next person. This, too, was the opposite of what he was used to in school. Instead of requiring a minimum number of pages, which carried with it the message that reading was something to be avoided, I'd set a maximum, which implied that it was desirable. It also gave him some control over how much he read. He could begin with a very short story and move up if he wished.

I began by reading one of the stories, using outrageous voices for the different characters and a very solemn voice for the narrator. I stumbled a few times (not on purpose), but brushed those mistakes off. When it was the boy's turn to read, he was nervous. I reminded him that what was most important was to use different voices. If he came to a word he was having trouble reading, he should just replace it with a word he knew that would make sense. (That would not only make running across an unfamiliar word less disturbing, but would increase the likelihood of his actually figuring it out, because he'd be paying more attention to the story as a whole.)

He began timidly. I stopped him and said that he was using his normal voice. He had to figure out what the narrator would sound like. Did he want it to be an old man with a craggy voice, a little girl, or even possibly a snake? He thought about that for a moment, and then chose a character.

He quickly got the hang of it, and by the end of the evening he was reading stories with new confidence, using different voices for each character. He no longer panicked when he saw an unfamiliar word. Instead, he'd pause and figure out what word would make sense in that situation.

We read aloud to each other every evening for the rest of the week. On Friday morning the boy came over to his mother after breakfast and told her that he wanted to read a story aloud to her before he left for school. She was stunned. Not only had his reading improved after only a few days, but his attitude had changed. Reading was no longer something to be afraid of, it was fun. By the end of the school year his reading skills had caught up with and passed most of his classmates'.

I tell that story to show how, in most cases, children in early elementary school will get back on track with a semester or two of individual attention. Unfortunately, few teachers have the time to provide such individual attention, so it's up to parents.

Providing help at home doesn't necessarily mean rushing out and hiring a tutor. Two pieces of standard advice are to read children more bedtime stories and to place labels on some objects at home, such as chairs, to help children associate the written word with the physical object. But there are several other inexpensive and simple things that parents can do to help their children not fall further behind in reading skills. Some of these suggestions even contradict the advice given out when today's parents were learning to read.

Many children don't see how reading fits in with their other activities. Few of the books given to beginning readers are intrinsically interesting, especially when compared with what's on television. Since most children's level of sophistication far outstrips their ability to read, they have little incentive to struggle through simple tales and awkward rhymes. They have no emotional investment in the plots of their primers.

But a child who's having trouble reading a page in a workbook may be more motivated to read a note her mother has packed in her lunch box. That type of reading practice is much more fun and inherently rewarding. It turns reading into a bond between the parent and the child instead of a potentially divisive issue.

Also, children (and parents, for that matter) are more likely to read material that addresses their developmental and emotional needs as well as their struggles for power and recognition. While adults may turn to the latest romance novel or thriller for the same effect, young children are drawn to a different source. It's a body of literature that's been shunned by both parents and educators for years: comic books.

According to Jim Trelease, who has written several books on helping children become good readers, studies have found that 90 percent of students in top reading groups are or were avid comic-book readers who graduated to more complicated books as they grew older. (Trelease claims to have had the largest comic-book collection in his neighborhood when he was growing up.)

Schools have used a variety of approaches to teach reading to children over the past fifty years, with different ones passing in and out of vogue. The underlying problem has been that not all children learn best from the same approach. For example, about 10 percent of children, according to some experts, have difficulty learning to read phonetically. These are the same children who have a lot of trouble learning to spell.

Like my friend's son, whom I described a few pages back, they'll look pained or even fearful when they try to sound out an unfamiliar word. They'll lose track of where they are in a story. It's a problem that seems to run in families.

While listening to an adult read aloud helps all children learn to read, it's especially useful for these children. The more stories they hear, the better they become at predicting what words an author may use in a particular situation. That experience helps them narrow down the alternatives when they're trying to figure out a new or complex word.

ENCOURAGING YOUR CHILD TO READ

One of the best predictors of how well children will read is how much their parents read. The children who have the most trouble in elementary school tend to have parents who didn't read to them when they were younger and didn't play word games with them. They also tend to have less experience seeing the adults around them reading and writing.

Having said that, it's important to realize that some children from highly literary and educated homes have trouble learning to read. Here are some things that can help:

- Jim Trelease, the reading guru, wisely recommends that parents give their children four gifts. The first two, a library card and one's own books, are treasured signs of a child's growing maturity.[5] The third is a book basket for the kitchen so that children can read when they're eating a snack. Children often want to read when they're eating alone. That's why one of the most widely read items in a home is the back of a cereal box.

   Finally, buy your child a bed lamp and let him stay up a bit later to read in bed. It's probably the most important night school your child will ever attend.

- Encourage your child to participate in the reading and writing you do at home. Read things aloud that interest you. It may be a short article from a newspaper or magazine, or even a joke. Play word games together. Encourage your child to contribute to the letters you write, even if she only writes a sentence or two. Have your child add

---

[5] I still have the first book I was ever given, and distinctly remember getting my first library card. I remember sitting in the children's section of our local library and trying to write my name in what seemed like an impossibly small space on the application form. The rules have apparently eased up a bit. When my son got his first library card at age four, he simply had to show the librarian that he could write his first name on a sheet of paper.

items she wants to your shopping list. Those activities help her see the connection between the reading skills she's trying to master and other aspects of her life outside school.

• Keep in mind that success breeds confidence in children who are anxious about reading. Punishing children by forcing them to read or write a certain amount is counter-productive, for it teaches them to associate reading with anger and pain instead of pleasure. Pushing them to read books that are too complex has the same negative result.

Remember that there's no such thing as a book that's too easy if that book has substance. In elementary school, it's much more important that your child read anything than that he read from some list of classics. If he likes horses or knights in shining armor or music, help him find out where the books on those topics are kept in the local library. After all, as adults we read as a way of indulging our interests and fantasies. *Moby Dick* can wait.

PROBLEMS WITH MATHEMATICS

Mathematics may be the most anxiety-provoking subject taught. For many adults, especially those who avoided math in school, facing a column of numbers, a graph, or a set of fractions still makes their palms sweat and their heart race. In fact, many of today's math-anxious parents probably learned their fear from their own parents or elementary school teachers who also felt incompetent when it came to working with numbers. It is a cycle that, unfortunately, can be passed on to today's children as well. While I know of no evidence to show that math anxiety is genetic, it clearly seems to be contagious.

But if you look at toddlers, you'll find that they are generally fascinated by numbers. At that age, numbers offer predictability and, from that, power. It is an attitude that all too often changes when they reach elementary school.

Elementary school teachers usually receive far less training in how to teach mathematics than how to teach reading and writing. In fact, many selected their profession at least partly because they felt uncomfortable taking advanced college-level courses in mathematics or the sciences. They are likely to view mathematical ability as something they cannot expect from all children—a strikingly different attitude than the one they hold toward such subjects as reading and spelling.

The misconception that basic mathematical ability is innate often leads children and their parents to respond more passively to mathematics than to other subjects, waiting to discover whether they have a natural talent for it. There is less incentive to work hard at it because it feels out of their control. This leads some children and teachers to interpret a child's initial difficulty understanding something as an inability to master it.

The issue of math anxiety is significant for both children and parents. Comfort with and competence at mathematics are increasingly important for success in adulthood. Avoiding math courses severely restricts the fields a student can study and the jobs a new college graduate can find. Although it may seem a bit premature to worry about such things while your child's in elementary school, it isn't. Attitudes about mathematical competence form early. Bad experiences in the first few grades can have a domino effect, limiting a child's selection of courses in junior high school, high school, and so forth.

Although it's sometimes assumed that girls are more anxious about math than boys, and that students who do poorly in the subject are more anxious than those who do well, research has shown that's not the case. Many students who do well in math are still anxious, and attribute their success to luck instead of knowledge and effort. And while studies have found differences in math anxiety between boys and girls, they've been slight.

One source of anxiety about mathematics can clearly be traced to early classroom experiences. A woman I interviewed who teaches adults who are uncomfortable with numbers said that she would routinely notice students who hid their hands under their desks as soon as she asked them to do a problem out loud. Few were conscious of the habit. When she explored further, she found that almost all of these adults had attended parochial elementary school. Back then, many of the nuns who taught would rap young students on the knuckles with a ruler if they gave an incorrect answer. Unfortunately, what the students had learned and carried with them to adulthood was fear, not arithmetic.

HELPING OUT WITH MATH PROBLEMS

Children look to their parents for cues as to how they should respond when they're frustrated by a math problem. The parents' attitudes when facing their own math problems at home are often much more important than their ability to "crunch numbers." A parent who shows her children the process of pondering the question, drawing a diagram or two to clarify the problem, approximating the answer, and then doing the calculations will help her children more than one who does it in her head or out of sight of her children. Though the first approach may take longer, it teaches persistence and other important skills. It also shows a child what may be new ways of looking at math problems.

If your child is anxious about mathematics, here are some other things you can do:

- Pay attention to your own feelings about mathematics. Are you anxious? Do you treat your child's math homework differently than that of other subjects? Children sense their parents' attitudes and quickly learn whether they are expected to succeed or fail.

- All too often, the math problems children are asked to solve in school seem irrelevant. Have you ever really needed to know how far apart two trains are an hour and a half after they leave the station? When was the last time you wanted to know how many rods there were in the perimeter of a field?

If you'd like your child to practice solving problems, choose ones that fit his interests. Calculate baseball batting averages. Figure out how many pieces of candy he can buy for a given amount of money. You can also show how mathematics is embedded in newspaper stories and advertisements.

- Remember that, as with reading, success is critical to further success. Let your child feel comfortable with each basic skill, such as division, before moving on. Otherwise you're setting your child up for frustration and failure.

FAILING AT SCHOOL

There's no easy answer to how you should respond when your child brings home a failing grade on a report card or a note from a teacher warning of academic problems. Unplugging the television set, hiring a tutor, or arranging for summer school can help in some cases, but can be ineffective or even counterproductive in others. The most important first step is to find out why your child is failing. It's a good idea to begin by asking your child. Then ask the teacher. Only rarely will they tell you exactly the same thing.

Figuring out why a child is having trouble at school, especially if that child is clearly capable of doing the work, can be difficult. Knee-jerk reactions, like blaming the teacher or insisting that your child simply work harder, are seldom useful.

Among children in late elementary school, an overall decline in grades—especially a sharp decline—generally indicates a problem outside of school. Suddenly failing a class can be a cry for help with difficulties at home, such as an impending divorce or the stress of a sibling's life-threatening illness. It may signal social problems that parents and teachers have overlooked, such as being teased extensively by classmates and not knowing how to handle it.

A failing grade in early elementary school may be a sign of a deficit in a basic academic skill like reading, or even a medical problem like poor vision or hearing. Some children have difficulty sitting still for the increasing amounts of time required as they pass through the early grades. Their inability to focus their efforts may be a sign of an attention-deficit disorder.[6]

A slow decline in grades usually tells a different story and signals a need for remedial help, such as tutoring. When done well, tutoring can be remarkably effective for many children because it changes the context of learning. The individual attention of a tutor allows a child to learn more rapidly than in a normal classroom setting, and helps build confidence in handling academic material—confidence that can transfer to the classroom as well. A child who's several months behind his peers in arithmetic may be able to catch up in a much shorter time.

FINDING A TUTOR

Parents searching for tutors for their children often find that it's feast or famine. In some areas of the country, especially large cities, they have their choice of everything from franchised tutoring businesses to unemployed teachers to graduate students looking to make a few extra dollars. In other places the choices are slim, often limited to a local high

---

[6] Attention-deficit disorder (ADD) and attention-deficit–hyperactivity disorder (ADHD) have recently become "fashionable" diagnoses in the United States. The effect of the fashion can be seen, for example, in the rate of diagnosis of ADD and ADHD in the United States being approximately *double* that in Great Britain. There's no biological reason for such a dramatic difference, of course. It seems that many of the children diagnosed in the United States are behaving in ways that other countries would consider within the range of normal.

If you're concerned that your child may have ADD or ADHD, it's important that an assessment of him be made by a thoroughly trained child psychiatrist or child psychologist in conjunction with your pediatrician or family physician.

school student or a teacher doing a little moonlighting. Here are some suggestions for finding and working with a tutor:

- Don't try to do the tutoring yourself. This is different from helping your child prepare for a test or figure out how to do some homework. By the time a child needs tutoring, odds are the subject has become an emotionally charged issue in your family. That overlay of emotion means that parents very seldom do as good a job of tutoring their own children as an outsider can.

- Use the grapevine. Begin by talking to your child's teachers and to other parents about tutors they have worked with. Don't be too impressed by academic credentials or advanced degrees. A sensitive and talented high school or college student can sometimes do a very effective job.

- Do your homework as a parent. If possible, ask to watch at least part of a session when a tutor works with a child who is your child's age. Talk to the parents of other children the tutor has worked with. Remember that most children approach being tutored with trepidation. Will they fail again? Does this mean they're simply stupid? Good tutors are very sensitive to those fears and begin by building a relationship with the student.

- Ask how the tutor will determine the underlying problem. Sometimes the child's regular teacher or school psychologist has already done this and can pass that information along. For example, a child who's having trouble understanding fractions may have missed some fundamental concepts of multiplication and division. Simply drilling that child on fractions will only increase his frustration and may lead to failure. Instead, the tutor should have the child backtrack to the point at which he's mastered the necessary arithmetic skills, and then move forward.

- Stay involved. Don't send your child to a tutor as if you were dropping off your car at the garage for a tune-up.

Ask what you can do to help at home. Bear in mind, however, that there are times when the best thing you can do is leave your child alone for a while. This is especially true if schoolwork has become a bone of contention between you and your child, and he's feeling a lot of pressure from you to succeed. By backing off and leaving the tutoring to an outside person, your child is likely to feel more comfortable and to do better.

CHEATING IN SCHOOL

I once interviewed the principal of an elementary school in the Midwest who had just had a talk with a ten-year-old boy. The boy had been caught cheating, having come to class with the answers to a standardized test written on the backs of his hands. He'd copied some of the questions from the test booklet the day before the examination. The principal told me that the boy was feeling pressure from home to score well. The cheating was a sign that the child was having difficulty with his parents' expectations of him.

Studies of children who cheat at school indicate that the boy may simply have been precocious, not unusual.[7] Cheating is quite rare in the early grades, in part because students are still mastering basic skills, such as reading and writing, that they'll need if they are to cheat. Also, some young children simply don't understand that it's wrong to cheat. The concept may be too sophisticated for them, although they clearly recognize that it's a good idea to get high grades on a test or essay.

Parents who receive word from school that their child has cheated sometimes have conflicting reactions to the news. Their

[7] Surveys of young adults have found that more than 70 percent admit to having cheated at least once during high school. Studies of cheating at large state universities found that between 50 and 60 percent of students admitted to having cheated during their first two years.

concern may be tempered with a bit of pride if they hear, for example, that their child has been called to the principal's office for punching a classmate who'd been taunting him.[8]

A call or a note from a teacher saying that a child has been caught cheating, however, brings about a very different emotional response. Parents almost always see a covert behavior, such as cheating or lying, as more serious than outright aggression, such as punching another child. Unlike the bruises and other telltale signs of schoolyard fights, cheating offers no easy way for parents to know if the problem has continued. Because of this, parents are far more likely to remain suspicious for months after the incident.

From a young child's perspective, however, isolated instances of cheating are simply expedient solutions to a problem. It is a way for him to meet what he perceives as impossible expectations from the adults in his life. Any ethical considerations are buried by the pressures he's feeling.

RESPONDING TO A CHEATING INCIDENT

If you get that dreaded call from a school saying that your child has been caught cheating, here are some things you can do:

- Let your child know where you stand on cheating. Keep in mind that children in the second or third grade may

---

[8] I remember being in this situation in the sixth grade. After giving a series of escalating warnings (although I didn't use that term at the time) to a bully in my class who'd been throwing pieces of wood at me in shop class, I picked up a baseball-sized piece he'd tossed and flung it back. By chance, it hit him in the eye. He had to be taken to the emergency room. (He suffered no permanent damage.) I was sent to the principal's office.

The principal listened to my story and told me what I'd done was wrong. You know the speech: "You should have gone to the teacher." (I had.) "Two wrongs don't make a right." (True enough, but neither does being bullied.) Then, after thinking a moment, she admitted that she might very well have done the same thing had she been in my situation. When I got home that afternoon, my mother had already heard from the principal. She told me that what I'd done was wrong, but that she was very proud of me.

assume that you'd like them to get good marks any way they can. Children this age may not understand that what they're doing is wrong.

You should also look at your own behaviors as well as your words. Children who overhear adults in their family discussing income they didn't declare on their tax returns or how they talked their way out of speeding tickets may assume that cheating at school is an equally creative and appropriate way of getting what they want.

- Don't simply punish your child for cheating. Doing that alone may, in fact, trigger more cheating, for it undermines a child's self-concept and doesn't teach him what he needs to know to accomplish his goals in other ways.

  You should follow up any punishment with help in developing ways of doing well at school without cheating. Work with your child on developing more effective study habits. Go over ways of breaking down and tackling an assignment.

- Ask your child why he felt he needed to cheat. Odds are you won't get a straight answer to this question, at least at first. Your child will, quite naturally, be defensive. But if you're patient you may be able to learn about some of the pressures he has been feeling but has been unable to express directly. Does he believe you expect perfect performance from him? Does he need more help organizing his life so that he has time to study?

- Ask yourself and your child's teacher if this incident is part of a larger pattern of dishonesty. Has your child also been lying or stealing recently? Has he been completing his other assignments? If the cheating is an isolated incident, just talking about it can often solve the problem. But if the cheating is part of a larger pattern, it's a good idea to seek out some professional help.

GIFTED CHILDREN

It may seem odd at first to think of being academically or intellectually gifted as a problem. Obviously the giftedness itself isn't the issue. Rather, it's whether a gifted child's intellectual and emotional needs are being met at school and at home.

I remember interviewing a professor of psychology who was conducting a major study on academically gifted children. She recalled feeling shocked a few years earlier when she received a call from the principal of her eight-year-old son's school saying that the boy was failing arithmetic. (One reason for her shock was that he had started kindergarten two years early because he was generally academically gifted and had special talents in mathematics.)

When she spoke to the teacher, she discovered that her son was doing extremely well on his examinations but wasn't bothering to do the homework assignments, which he found boring. She solved the child's (and the school's) problem by using a two-pronged approach. She persuaded her son to do his homework to keep the school happy. She also hired a college student to teach him algebra so that he'd feel challenged instead of bored.

Academically gifted children—usually defined as those who score in the top 2 to 5 percent nationally according to some measure, often an intelligence or achievement test—face special problems. So do their parents. Schools treat these children differently from those whose talents lie in other areas, like music, art, and sports. Being academically gifted is a topic laced with myths and fears, many of which are unfounded.

Contrast what happens to academically gifted versus athletically gifted children. Most of the athletes are allowed to develop their special skills at whatever rate best suits them, and no one gives it a second thought. No one tries to stop them from becoming much better baseball players or swimmers than their classmates.

Yet if an academically gifted child tries to do two years of work in one, that's viewed as potentially harmful. Much of the concern focuses on the nonacademic areas of these gifted children's development. Will they feel out of place among older children? Can they handle the social pressure?

Researchers emphasize that for the vast majority of academically gifted children, those concerns are groundless. In fact, these children are more likely to develop social and even academic problems if they *don't* feel intellectually challenged. But problems are often overlooked because they can be working far below their potential and still be at the tops of their classes.

This sometimes leads to another hidden problem, which can take years to appear. If gifted children don't go to challenging programs, they may not learn how to learn. Eventually, in college or graduate school, they feel emotionally overwhelmed when they can't just coast through their courses anymore.

For other children, the academic and emotional problems come earlier. Boys in elementary school who are bored tend to act up in class and be labeled as troublemakers, even though their grades are high. Because their behavior annoys teachers, they're more likely to be referred for help.

Girls of that age in the same situation are likely to be highly cooperative, even though they're putting very little effort into their work. Teachers and parents assume that everything is fine because they're causing little trouble. But when they reach high school and get their first "B" in a class, they sometimes become depressed and may even stop working altogether.[9]

Academically gifted children who feel intellectually challenged, who are allowed to proceed at their own rates, and who feel emotionally supported are less likely to show any of those problems. Remember that one of the greatest sources of frustration for both children and adults is the feeling that you were never able to work up to your potential.

---

[9] A colleague of mine who runs a clinic for underachieving students tells me that 90 percent of the children she sees in elementary school are boys. Among high school students, only 50 percent of the children she sees are boys.

HELPING GIFTED CHILDREN ACHIEVE

There is no single best way to help gifted children reach their potential. In fact, the criteria for giftedness are somewhat arbitrary and, according to many researchers, far too narrow.[10] If you've been told that your child is gifted, here are some things to keep in mind:

- Make sure any program you're considering meets your child's needs, not your own. While a child's giftedness does reflect well on her parents, that can turn into a problem if those parents push their child so that *they* look good. This is seldom done consciously, of course. But you should always ask yourself if you're enrolling your child in a special program for her benefit or for other reasons.

- Recognize that you and your child have several options, even if your school system doesn't have special programs for gifted children. These include early admission into kindergarten, moving to a higher grade during the day to study a certain subject, and skipping one or more grades entirely. Parents sometimes circumvent the strict age requirements that many public schools have for entry into kindergarten by enrolling children early in private or parochial schools for a year or two, and then switching to public schools.

- Remember that some children are reluctant at first to participate in special programs. Encourage them to try. Children harbor many of the same anxieties as adults about

---

[10] For example, Dr. David Henry Feldman, a professor of developmental psychology at Tufts University and one of the leading researchers in this field, says that it's a mistake to limit our notion of giftedness to traditional academic skills. It should also include such areas as art, leadership, sensitivity to others, and other special talents.

being academically gifted. They worry that the label will act as a barrier between them and their friends.

This problem tends to be worse with girls, who will often hide their talents because they feel that if they look too bright, they will find themselves lonely and socially isolated. That fear is usually unwarranted.'' After a few weeks, they often find themselves more comfortable with their new classmates than with their old ones.

- Schedule regular meetings with the teachers in your child's gifted program. Make sure your discussions cover not only the academic progress your child is making, but also how she's handling things emotionally.

- Don't be surprised at how quickly your child can learn. It's not unusual for gifted students to learn an entire year or even two of a subject during an intensive summer program. This shows how inappropriate the standard curriculum is for these children.

'' Sometimes it isn't. When my wife was in the sixth grade in Minnesota, she was placed in a special (and poorly conceived) one-year gifted program that contained children from all of the elementary schools in her city. She hated it, largely because it made her sever her social relationships with her long-established friends. She also was teased about being "a brain" by the kids in her neighborhood because she had to ride a special bus to get to her school. The program provided no counseling or other support services to the students.

Things went much better when she moved on to a junior high school that didn't have a gifted program. She didn't feel as conspicuous simply going across the street to the senior high school to take mathematics classes.

3

The Connection Between School and Home

Education is what remains when we have forgotten all that we have been taught.
                    —GEORGE SAVILE, LORD HALIFAX (1633–1695)

The reason for parents to get involved in their children's education is simple: the effort is an excellent long-term investment. Children whose parents stay informed and influential in their children's schools do better academically and socially than children whose parents do not. Parental involvement in elementary school is a way of telling your children that you value the work they're doing and the efforts they're making.

Yet for much of this century, school was a world children seldom shared with their parents, who mostly caught oblique glimpses through report cards and essays, pageants and PTA meetings. Parents were often kept at bay by an unwritten but generally accepted school policy that discouraged parents from becoming too involved with such critical issues as the curriculum. Those parents who tried to buck the system a generation ago were seen as domineering or pushy. Unless they had credentials as educators themselves, their suggestions were often politely but firmly dismissed.

We can see this attitude in the image of the school volunteer from thirty years ago. A volunteer was almost always a mother who baked brownies, accompanied classes on field trips, or ran the book sale—tasks which sound impractical if not impossible to many of today's two-career or single-parent families. Her involvement was limited to peripheral issues rather than issues central to the running of the school.

All this has changed in many school districts.[1] A growing number now welcome parents' participation more enthusiastically than ever before. Administrators see parental involvement as a matter of both practical pedagogy and economic reality, as many schools face larger tasks with smaller budgets. Today's teachers are far more receptive to parents' involvement than they used to be.

Even so, many parents and teachers still harbor misconceptions about their respective roles and how they can work together. Parents—especially those who have less education than their children's teachers—sometimes feel uncomfortable talking with teachers as partners. It is as if, by entering the building, they have once again become students in an inherently unequal relationship with the teachers and administration.

Also, teachers may falsely assume that single parents and dual-career couples are uninterested or unable to participate in school activities. Studies have found that this simply isn't true. On average, single mothers are at least as involved in their children's schoolwork as other mothers. They're less involved in matters that require visiting the school, however, because they don't have as much time available, especially during regular school hours.

---

[1] Not all school districts, unfortunately. As I was writing this chapter I noticed a newspaper article about an elementary school in Queens, New York, at which the administration painted a red line on the sidewalk outside the school and told parents that they could not cross it. I was amazed! My first thought was that I should go out there, tell them I was a parent of one of their students, and cross the line, just to see what the administration did.

GETTING INVOLVED WITH
YOUR CHILD'S SCHOOL

One challenge for today's parents is finding effective and appropriate ways of participating in our children's schools. According to Dr. Joyce L. Epstein, the co-director of the Center on Families, Communities, Schools, and Children's Learning at Johns Hopkins University in Baltimore, the essence of parental involvement is finding ways of supporting the school's goals and children's learning anyplace and anytime.

Here are some suggestions:

- Encourage schools to adapt parent-teacher communications to the schedules and needs of today's parents. For example, a few very creative schools are holding parent-teacher conferences by sending the teachers to the students' homes. This is, of course, much more easily done in elementary school, since one teacher handles most or all of a child's academic subjects.

  I'm a big fan of this approach for several reasons. It lets teachers know much more about a child's home environment than they'd get from an interview at school. It makes it more convenient for the parents, who don't have to arrange for child care so that they can attend a conference at school. Finally, it means that parents don't have to feel rushed because someone else is waiting for the teacher's attention.

  The major problem with this approach is that it takes much more time than traditional conferences. Then again, who said that education had to be efficient?

  An alternative to this, which I also strongly endorse, is to invite your child's teachers to your home for part of an afternoon or an evening toward the beginning of the school year. You don't have to worry about making a formal dinner. Coffee or tea will do. Use the time to find out about each other as adults, and to look into ways of jointly helping your child and her classmates grow as students.

- Set up telephone conferences in between formal meetings. Find out when your child's teachers have free periods, and arrange to speak with them by phone at those times. Remember that your child doesn't have to be having difficulties for you to speak with her teacher.

- Ask your children specific questions about what they're doing in school. Simply asking "How was your day at school, dear?" probably won't yield any useful information. Children love it if you ask them about the important details of their lives at school, such as how things went with the social studies presentation that they'd mentioned the day before, or whether they got to play kickball again in gym class. That attention to detail shows that you're really listening and value what they have to say.

DISAGREEMENTS WITH A TEACHER

It took a few years before a friend of mine came to terms with the bitterness she felt toward her daughter's fifth-grade teacher. The girl has a slight hearing impairment. The mother repeatedly tried to get the girl's teacher to take that into account and to make sure her daughter heard the homework assignments, but to no avail.

The girl was having much more trouble hearing in this teacher's class than she'd had in any other. Her academic work suffered, along with her self-image. Her mother met with the teacher, the principal, and the school social worker, but nothing changed. The problem disappeared the next year when the girl was assigned to a new teacher. My friend feels that the fifth grade was a wasted year for her daughter.

All parents will, at some point, object to something that is happening to their children at school. If the problem is clear-cut, as when a teacher hits a child or writes scathing personal comments on his papers, we act without hesitation to ensure his safety and correct the problem. Our response is automatic and unquestioned.

Yet many parents have second thoughts about interceding when the problem is more subtle. What do we do if our child feels ignored in class, or if we suspect that a teacher is prejudiced against him? This time there are no outward signs or documents to support our claims. Will raising objections further jeopardize our child by labeling him (and us) as troublemakers? Will our competence and authority as parents be questioned? Will a disagreement teach our children to disrespect and disobey their teachers?

Children—even those in elementary school—can learn a lot from how their parents handle these issues. It's important for children to understand that it's normal for people to disagree about rules and decisions, and that people can resolve their differences.

Even so, the discomfort many parents feel when they enter a school is palpable.[2] Unfortunately, this discomfort often leads to taking an extreme approach by becoming passive or inappropriately hostile. It's important that you pay close attention to your feelings when faced with this situation. Disagreeing with your child's teacher can stir up surprisingly strong emotions—the source of which may have little to do with the current situation and a lot to do with our own experiences as students. They may even be replays of battles we've had with our parents.

---

[2] I still remember how, on a visit to my high school, I stopped for a few moments before walking through the doors to the teachers' lounge. All the cues from the environment—the sights, sounds, and smells, that had surrounded me when I was a student there—told me that this was a place I shouldn't enter. At the time of this visit I was in my thirties, and therefore older than some of the teachers. I was also a professor at a large university. Still, those old feelings held me back. When I finally walked into the teachers' lounge, I half expected one of them to throw me out.

ACTING AS YOUR CHILD'S ADVOCATE

There are several things you can do to improve the odds of successfully resolving a conflict with one of your child's teachers:

• Get involved with your child's school *before* there's a problem. The parents who are most successful at complaining to a teacher or principal are those who've been regularly involved in school activities through the PTA and by attending parent-teacher conferences. Teachers and administrators are more likely to listen to someone they already know from more pleasant circumstances.

• Don't jump in at the first sign of trouble. Remember that students in the upper grades of elementary school often complain about their teachers at the beginning of a new school year. It can be a way for your children to let you know how much effort they're putting into school this year.

   First, give your child and the teacher time to get used to each other's needs and personal styles. Next, if your child is in one of the upper grades, talk to him about how he might be able to resolve the problem himself, such as by asking for extra help. If that doesn't work, set up a meeting with the teacher.

• Begin by gathering information from the school as well as from your child. Sometimes children misinterpret why teachers are doing something. A teacher may view the opportunity to do some extra or advanced work on a topic as an honor and a privilege. The student may view being singled out from his peers as a form of punishment.

• Don't belittle a teacher in front of your child. Aside from being rude, doing so puts children in an awkward situation. Even those children who complain loudly about specific teachers have mixed feelings about them. Children who hear their teachers being denigrated by their parents will feel belittled as well.

- Share information with the teacher about your child's behavior at home, and ask what's happening at school. There are several reasons for this. First, it avoids putting the teacher on the defensive, as would have happened had you begun with a complaint about something she's doing. You're also helping the teacher gain a better perspective on your child. Finally, you may discover some important things that are going on which your child hasn't told you. (Perhaps the *real* reason she asked him to redo his arithmetic homework was because he never handed it in, not because, as your child put it, "She's just mean!")

- Don't be intimidated. School rules and educational theories are sometimes arcane and confusing, even to people in the profession. Find out from your children's teachers the rationale behind any decisions you question. If you don't understand the jargon a teacher is using, ask for an explanation before you go any further.

- Be assertive with the teacher without being aggressive. Pushiness from either party is likely to backfire, since it will make the other person more defensive and more entrenched in his or her position. No one likes to be told how to behave.

    Instead, approach the problem like a diplomat. Remember that each of you is seeing your child from a different perspective. Share those views. Talk about what you can each do to help your child succeed in school.

- If nothing helps, move up the hierarchy. The administrative structure of a school district is often as rigid as that of the military. You'll usually get a better response if you try to talk to the school's guidance counselors and principal before complaining to the superintendent's office.

Remember that you can always ask to have your child placed in another classroom, but you should do that only as a last resort. Changing classrooms may unintentionally give your child the message that there's something fundamentally wrong with him and add to the stress he's feeling.

HOMEWORK

A few years ago, I interviewed an educational consultant in California who'd noticed that his fourth-grade son was having a lot of trouble completing what should have been a routine homework assignment. When the boy asked for help, the father looked at the son's textbook and discovered that all the answers he needed were in one chapter. He pointed this out to his son, who replied, "The teacher said to answer the questions. She didn't say we had to read the chapter, too!"

To many children, homework is regarded as little more than a curse. They ignore, avoid, forget, or rush through it with obvious distaste. It's little wonder why. Most homework assigned in elementary school consists of drills and worksheets, with no obvious connection to the child's life and needs outside of school. Even the reasons behind more creative homework assignments, such as writing a book report, are unclear to most children. Is it a test of whether she actually read the book, or a request for her opinion and analysis?

Researchers have recently begun paying increased attention to the effect of homework in elementary school on children's later academic success. Although most public schools don't begin assigning regular homework until the fifth or sixth grade, there's strong evidence that children who do homework in the earlier grades tend to do better as they progress through school. A child who's hit with her first serious homework assignment in junior high school—something that happens all too often—will probably have a lot of difficulty breaking the task into components and organizing her work.

The usefulness of early homework doesn't mean that a second grader should have to stay up late completing worksheets of subtraction problems. One good rule of thumb is that students should spend about ten minutes per grade level studying on weekdays. Thus, a first grader should have about ten minutes of homework per night; a sixth grader should have about an hour. If your child has little or no homework assigned, she should spend that time studying. (This also helps her avoid the temptation to rush through her arithmetic problems—"See, Mom, I'm finished!"—so that she can watch her favorite television program.)[3]

Knowing when and how to help your children with their school projects and homework is as much an art as a science. The things they learn from your involvement often have more to do with their self-image and your relationship than with the topic of the assignment. Ideally, by working together you can help improve their skills and reinforce the value you put on schoolwork.

Children under ten years of age usually require a lot of involvement—but not necessarily help—from their parents. Much of that involvement focuses on the mechanics of homework: reminding them of their study time, checking their assignments, and sometimes even sitting down with them to make sure they get started.

While it's important that you stay involved, you have to stop short of going too far by actually doing your child's assignments. (After all, do you really need to repeat the fourth grade?) While almost always well-intentioned, doing a homework assignment for a child can backfire, because it gives her the message that she's fundamentally incompetent and will not be able to do this type of work on her own. Instead, you should respect your child's need to struggle with problems and master them. If you find, however, that

---

[3] Your expectations for how a first grader should study will, of course, be significantly different from what you'd expect from a sixth grader. For a younger child, studying can be making a drawing (practicing fine motor skills). An older child could spend the time reading a book or reviewing for a test.

your child simply can't do the assignment or is totally baffled by it, call up her teacher immediately so that the underlying problem doesn't get any worse.

When you assume the role of a homework coach, bear in mind that your child will be very sensitive to what you say. In fact, your child wants to please you so much that she'll react much more dramatically to your criticism than to the same criticism from her teacher. (If you'd like an analogy, think about getting feedback on your driving skills or tennis game from your spouse as opposed to a professional instructor.)

Although it may be tempting to rush in with help when you see your child is having trouble, try not to do so. Instead, let your child know that you're available if she wants you. Let her control whether, when, and how she asks for your help.

For children in early elementary school, the best support may involve little more than giving them healthful meals (it's hard to concentrate if your stomach's empty) and a quiet place to work, and praising them while reading over or listening to their homework. When they're slightly older and more accomplished, you can offer specific advice and, when appropriate, quiz them on material they're trying to master.

When children ask for help, gentle support and encouragement are more effective than pointing out all the things they could improve. It's important to let them "own" the project, even though you could do a better job. During the first few grades especially, you may feel compelled to correct a misspelled word on her writing assignment, but it's almost always better not to make the change.[4] Remember, your goal is to have your child come away from showing you her homework believing that she's successful and accepted by you. By overlooking the minor mistakes and focusing on her larger accomplishments, you'll help her gain the confidence she needs to take on more complicated tasks as she moves through school.

---

[4] This doesn't mean you should never pay attention to or correct her spelling or grammar. But in these early years, these details are less important than the task of organizing and writing down her thoughts.

HELPING WITH HOMEWORK

If your child is having difficulty with homework, or if you find that the two of you are fighting over it, here are some other approaches and techniques that might help:

- Don't try to be your child's teacher at home. Instead, become her student. Let your child teach you what she's trying to learn. That not only helps her master the material, but gives her a much-needed sense of power that's usually missing when she's in school. Besides, as any teacher will tell you, one of the best ways to learn a subject is to teach it.

- Change tactics. If the approach you've been using to help your child isn't working, own up to that fact and alter your own behavior first. One sign of a problem is if you find yourself saying something like, "If I've told you once, I've told you a thousand times . . ." After all, if that's true, then you have absolutely no reason to believe that the thousand-and-first time will be any different!

  In many families this situation calls for stopping such predictably futile approaches as criticizing your child for being lazy and warning her about the dire long-term consequences of not handing in her homework. Such harangues are almost always a sign that the discussions have deteriorated into a power struggle that the child is winning: she's exercising her control by *not* doing her homework.

- Don't banish your child to Siberia to do her homework. Many children are asked to do homework in depressing isolation. They're sent to their rooms and, in essence, told not to come down until they're through. Unfortunately, that means that children get the most attention from you when they *stop* studying and have to be told to go back. It also sends the message that homework is drudgery or perhaps a form of punishment, rather than a routine part of daily life.

Instead, try a different approach. Think of homework time as a social situation. Visit your child while she's in her room, or let her use the kitchen table to do homework if the environment is quiet enough. Bring her something to drink or make her a snack. Give her a quick neck rub or shoulder massage if she's working hard. All of these things show your support of her efforts and mean that she doesn't have to stop what she's doing to get your attention.

- Help your child see the connection between schoolwork and real life. Fractions and ratios are more fun and make more sense when you practice them by baking cookies together. History can be given a new relevance if you talk about the news. English composition can be more rewarding if you write each other letters.

- Don't reward procrastination. Although it's painful to watch children fail, sometimes it's the best thing a parent can do for them. If your child has put off an assignment until the last minute, don't jump in and rescue her. Instead, let her see and feel the consequences of her mistakes. Next time, help her plan her time more appropriately.[5]

SCHOOL AVOIDANCE

A friend of mine vividly recalls how, when he was growing up in Brooklyn, he was picked on by a group of boys when he attended

---

[5] In some children, chronic procrastination can be a sign of perfectionism, which requires additional help. I'll deal with that shortly.

a new school. My friend decided to solve the problem by pretending to be sick so that he could stay home.

First thing in the morning he complained to his mother that he was feeling hot, and mentioned some other vague symptoms as well. Just as he'd predicted, she put a thermometer under his tongue and left the room for a few minutes. He took the thermometer out and placed it on his bedroom radiator.

His scheme worked for four days. On the fifth day he accidentally left his thermometer on the radiator too long. His mother didn't believe he had a temperature of 108°F, and sent him to school. (Her action was commendable. My friend overcame his fear and eventually became a child psychologist at Harvard.)

School avoidance—also known as school phobia or school refusal—is remarkably common.[6] We most often see it in two age groups: five- to seven-year-olds and twelve- to fourteen-year-olds. The intensity of the children's symptoms reflects their anxieties. Having a stomachache is an acceptable way for a child to substitute a predictable pain for a situation in which he feels out of control. For most children, their natural resilience takes over and they're back in school after a day or two at home.

For other children, however, the signs are much more serious. Instead of bouncing back, their time away from school increases their anxieties and, therefore, their symptoms. They get caught in a cycle of increasing fears and intensifying pains that are reinforced by staying away from school.

According to Dr. Barry Garfinkel, the former chief of child and adolescent psychiatry at the University of Minnesota, one out of every seven children will be absent from school for ten or more consecutive days for no medical reason before finishing high school. At any given time it affects about 3 percent of children. Approximately 60 percent of children who show this long-term school avoidance are clinically depressed and could use professional help.

---

[6] It's also one of the few mental health problems that appear equally among boys and girls. For almost every other diagnosis except eating disorders, boys have the problem more often than girls.

While school avoidance is most commonly triggered by situations at school such as a bully or a new class, it can also be brought about by events at home. For example, the death of a pet may cause some young children to wonder if their parents will also be dead when they return from school. The children may not be able to express that fear directly. Instead it comes out in their complaints of headaches which lead to their spending the day with the parent they worry might be lost.

Ironically, the failure of their unspoken fear to come true makes them more concerned instead of relieved. They figure that their being home is what protected their parents, so they must continue to feel sick.

Parents, too, are in a bind. If they're very nurturant and sympathetic during the episode, they're unintentionally reinforcing their child's behavior. If they yell at their child and accuse him of pretending to be sick, they'll raise his anxieties so that the intensity of his physical symptoms will increase.

HANDLING A CHILD WHO WON'T GO TO SCHOOL

So, how do you respond if your 7-year-old makes vague complaints about mysterious stomachaches and headaches, but your pediatrician can't find anything wrong? Here are some suggestions:

- Take the complaints seriously, even if you don't take them literally. Remember that a fear of school is a sign that something important and potentially destructive is happening in your child's life.

- Talk to your child not only about what's happening in school, but also what's happening on the way to and from school. Is there someone threatening him on the bus? Have other children been teasing him on the playground? Remember that some young children aren't afraid of school itself, but of being picked on in the common bathroom by older children, who choose that location to stay out of the sight of teachers.

You should also look at what changes have recently taken place at home that might be upsetting or frightening your child. Having a seriously ill grandparent can make a child worry (unrealistically) that if he goes to school he won't be available to save that person if there's a medical emergency. If his parents are considering a divorce, the child may view acting sick as the way to get them back together. Those underlying issues must be dealt with along with the school avoidance.

- Focus your talks on your child's emotions rather than what's frightening him. By acknowledging his feelings without criticizing them, you're reassuring him that you accept him even if he's frightened.

  Pay extra attention to your child's nonverbal signals. Instead of directly asking what he's afraid of, ask him what he did all day. Look for when his eyes avoid you or look down at the ground.

- If there's a real basis for his fears—a bully is extorting his milk money or older children are threatening him—talk to the teacher and the principal. School should be a safe haven for children.

- The bottom line in any treatment is that children have to go to school. According to Dr. Garfinkel, the only time a child should stay home is when he has a fever above 100°F or has an observable medical problem like a rash. And if your child's mystery illness clears up by midmorning, bring him to school at that time, rather than waiting until the next day.

PERFECTIONISM

A few years ago, while preparing a television report on perfection-ism in children, a photographer and I followed a five-year-old boy who was, to put it mildly, very easily frustrated. We videotaped him as he tried to build a house out of some small, interlocking plastic bricks. A few of the bricks stuck together. Instead of putting those aside or incorporating them into his building, he threw a kicking, screaming tantrum.

The boy was a perfectionist. Like others with that trait, he lived in a frightening and frustrating world of absolutes. Anything he did had to be "just so," or it was a failure and, by extension, he was a failure, too.

A typical elementary school class contains one or two children who are perfectionists—although few show the extreme behaviors of the child we videotaped. These are the children who get upset if their school papers are messy. If they make a mistake, they might insist on starting over. Unfortunately, this only increases their anx-iety and, consequently, the likelihood that they'll make more errors.

In the early grades they may be reluctant to try new skills or games, fearful that they will not be able to master them quickly enough to meet their personal standards. Sometimes they are re-luctant to write the alphabet for fear of getting it wrong. When they read aloud their voices are hesitant. They have difficulty play-ing with other children because their friends may not want to abide by the same rules.

In the later grades, perfectionistic children may be chronic pro-crastinators, who avoid working on homework assignments until the last minute. Some of these perfectionists get excellent—even perfect—grades in school. Others do consistently poorly and well below their intellectual abilities.

Therein lies the paradox of perfectionism. There's a perverse feeling of safety that comes from not studying for an imminent exam or not writing a book report until the evening before it's due. The child perfectionist feels that such work cannot be considered a true measure of his abilities. The incompleteness of his efforts allows him the fantasy that he could have done it perfectly if he'd only had the time. By not starting in a timely fashion, he puts off facing his fear.

We can see this in other realms of children's lives as well. Young girls who have eating disorders such as anorexia and bulimia are almost always perfectionists. They are in search of the perfect but unattainable body. As with all perfectionists, success is illusory.

Perfectionism tends to run in families, although we don't know whether it's caused by genes, the family environment, or some combination of factors. When I produced the videotape I mentioned earlier, I interviewed the five-year-old boy's mother. I asked her if anyone else in her family was a perfectionist. She thought long and hard about her answer before telling me that her father was a perfectionist and so was her brother. I asked her if, perhaps, she was a perfectionist. Again she pondered the question before answering. No, she told me, she wasn't good enough at it to be a perfectionist!

HELPING A CHILD WHO HAS TO GET EVERYTHING RIGHT

Many parents have mixed feelings about their children's perfectionistic tendencies—especially if they share that predisposition. After all, we want our children to aspire to excellence. Besides, not all children who are concerned with details are perfectionists.

One sign of a potential problem is if your child is chronically worried either about what she does or whether she'll be accepted by friends. Another sign of trouble is if she says she wants to stop, but can't. If either of these is true, it's a good idea to seek help from a child psychologist or psychiatrist. With these children, parents are seldom effective working alone. The emotional ties between you and your child are too strong.

For those children who seem just a bit too perfectionistic for their own good, there are some things you can do to help:

- Talk to a children's librarian about books for your child that deal with perfectionism. There are quite a few, each of which is tailored to a particular age. The stories can help your child get a better perspective on her feelings.

- Work with your child on study skills. Some young children, faced with their first book report, feel overwhelmed by the amount of organization the task requires. Everything seems equally important. Teach your child how to break an assignment down into its components and how to plan a schedule for completing it in manageable doses. That may give her the sense of control that she needs.

- Talk about some of your own fears and failures, both as an adult and as a child. Remember that young children tend to idealize their parents. Some may even assume that you've never made a mistake. One of the disadvantages of this naive belief is that your child may assume that she's not allowed to be imperfect. By talking about the time you failed a spelling test, lost a job or came in last in a race, you'll help her gain the realization that she, too, can make mistakes and survive them.

- Pay extra attention during significant changes in your child's life. Children with a tendency toward perfectionism often get particularly frustrated after a move to a new school or neighborhood. They don't know exactly what's expected of them by the new people in their lives. This is a time for additional reassurance.

- Look at your own perfectionistic behavior. Remember that children develop many of their attitudes and assumptions by watching their parents in ordinary situations. If you get upset over small problems or insist that things be done on a rigid timetable, those behaviors will outweigh anything you say to your child about how she should be calm and flexible.

WHEN NEATNESS BECOMES COMPULSIVE

Most cultures value neatness and drive in children. Parents encourage them to "stick with it" until they have finished a task. Teachers reward them for turning in neat papers and getting every answer right on a quiz. Most children gain a sense of mastery from putting together a jigsaw puzzle, painting a picture, or writing an essay.

But there are some children for whom orderliness is not enough. Their rooms are never quite tidy enough to suit them. Like perfectionists (with whom they share many traits), they may put off doing their homework until the last minute, then rush through it, claiming they could do better if only they'd had more time. These overly compulsive children usually need some professional help to break the cycle.

One way to tell if compulsivity is a problem is to ask if neatness, not the completion of a task, has become the objective. Instead of feeling masterful, compulsive children feel increasingly anxious. They lack the spontaneity and playfulness that we associate with school-age children. Instead, they worry about the future like a stockbroker who is worried about the next market crash.

Because parents expect and value a certain amount of diligence and persistence in a child, it is often difficult for parents to recognize when things have gone too far. One key is to look at whether the child's actions are appropriately matched to her age and stage of development. It's normal, for example, for toddlers to insist on drinking out of a special cup or to become upset if they do not hear the same story or song at bedtime. Their demands tell us that they realize that they can influence the world around them; they need not simply remain passive and accept it.

Preschoolers and children in early elementary school will often develop complex rules for the games they play. Indeed, some first graders may spend as much time negotiating the rules for a new game as they do playing it. Trying to account for all the possibilities helps them feel powerful and in control.

But when a child's need for order becomes too strong, it is because he feels powerless and out of control. At the extremes, highly compulsive children may become upset if they find a speck of dirt on their clothes, or they may spend hours each day counting objects or taking showers.

A psychologist I interviewed a few years ago told me about an eleven-year-old boy he had treated who was constantly drawing maps. If you asked him a questions about his vacation, for example, the boy would draw a map of where he and his family were, where they parked, the motel, and so forth. Each map took about half an hour to draw, and involved many erasures and corrections so that it would satisfy the boy. He would spend several hours a day drawing such maps. It interfered with his friendships, since other children, obviously, didn't find him much fun to be around. The maps were a strong metaphor for this boy's need to find his way in life. When he drew the maps, he wasn't anxious. He could control his fears.

While such behaviors are obvious signs of a problem, in many children who need help the symptoms are not as dramatic. What's most important is to look at whether the behavior is interfering with the child's schoolwork, social relationships, or play.

These extreme cases are rare—perhaps only about 1 percent of children—although many more have milder problems with rituals and neatness. Boys are slightly more likely than girls to have these problems in grade school. Older compulsive children are split evenly between boys and girls.

Trying to help these children can be very frustrating for parents. Simply telling them that their homework looks fine, for example, doesn't help. Instead, it convinces the children that their parents are not tuned in. They may become even more sure that they are not doing well enough, and increase their compulsive behavior.

The transition from being appropriately organized to being compulsive is almost always gradual, making it difficult for parents to describe when their children first began to have problems. In the rare instances when change in behavior occurs suddenly and dramatically, a thorough physical examination is called for, since such a sudden change may be a sign of a bacterial infection in the brain (this is extremely rare, but possible) or other physical illness.

The vast majority of anxious and compulsive children quickly respond to treatments that are much less dramatic. Behavior therapy and, if their anxieties are too overwhelming, a short course of medication to combat those anxieties help them feel back in control again.

LESSENING ANXIETIES ABOUT MISTAKES

Parents of obsessive-compulsive children often feel frustrated and alienated. If your child's behaviors are interfering with his life, you should seek outside professional help. Because of the intensity of the parent-child relationship, it's almost impossible to handle this problem alone.

But if the situation's not extreme, there are some things you can do to help a child who's merely a little anxious about making mistakes. Here are some suggestions:

• Take a hard look at other family members, including yourself. Compulsive behaviors, like perfectionism, tend to run in families. Ask yourself if you insist on having dinner at a particular time or on wearing perfectly clean clothes. How many mistakes has your child seen you make recently? Do you pay extra attention to your child when she does things neatly or has just had a bath?

In other words, look for ways you may be subtly and unconsciously encouraging your child's behavior. Many adults who have obsessive-compulsive behaviors recall how their parents were proud of insisting on a great deal of orderliness and cleanliness in their household.

- Remember that your child is grasping for a sense of control. A child may procrastinate and never finish his homework because all of his energy is going into largely irrelevant details, such as whether he has the right number of pencils. Parents may interpret this as a deliberate avoidance of schoolwork rather than seeing that the child is paralyzed by the need to make everything just right.

- Try to control your own anger and frustration over your child's behavior. This is more easily said than done, of course. Yelling at your child about the problem, however, will simply raise her anxieties. Instead, tell your child that you can see how uncomfortable these behaviors make her. That will make it easier to talk about and demonstrate some more efficient and appropriate ways that she can handle her anxieties.

4

Coping with Stress and Anxiety

Worry is interest paid on trouble before it falls due.
—W. R. INGE (1860–1954)

One sign of a child's maturity is the depth of her emotions. Infants and young toddlers often act as if they live in a black-and-white world. They are delighted or miserable and are intent upon letting you know their state of mind by offering up an infectious giggle or a heart-rending wail. By preschool, children see the grays in between the extremes as they develop empathy and begin to think about the future. This is when they first start to plan what they will be doing later in the day or even a few days hence, instead of concentrating only on the here and now. The growing subtlety of their feelings reflects their increasing ability to think.

Around age five those emotions begin to blossom into the full colors of the spectrum. The intensity of their feelings is now modulated by the situation. A spilled cup of juice or a torn art project is still upsetting, but is no longer treated as an earth-shaking event.[1]

---

[1] Unless, of course, the child is coming down with a cold. I noticed that, when my son was this age, a shift toward extreme emotions in response to minor prob-

That newfound sense of perspective is one of the markers of this stage of development. So is a school-age child's growing ability to use language to describe her emotions.[2]

A kindergartner, when asked what's troubling her, may need considerable prompting to identify the source of her distress. By the end of elementary school, making such connections is second nature to children. Still, there are many times when parents need to look beyond a child's words to figure out what's going on in that child's life and mind. That is one of the most challenging and most rewarding aspects of being a parent, for it helps solidify the bonds of understanding and attachment between us and our children.

A child's fears can give parents great insight into the challenges that child is struggling to master. At younger ages, those underlying issues are more readily apparent. A two-year-old is likely to be afraid of a thunderstorm or a growling dog. Those are concrete fears, for the objects are present at the time the child is afraid.

A four-year-old, however, will begin to worry about ghosts under the bed or monsters in the closet. Those are very different fears, for the monsters and ghosts are *not* present when the child is afraid. They are abstract fears. Their arrival should be a cause for celebration, for they show that the child is struggling to master the rudiments of abstract thought. They are a reflection of the development of his brain.

The shifts in predictable fears throughout elementary school also reflect a child's growing brain and changing situation. That's why it's important not to impose an adult's perspective on what children should or should not find frightening. A child who's anx-

---

lems and frustrations was a sure sign that he was on the verge of getting sick. His emotional lability would show up six to twelve hours before the first sniffle.

[2] This is the main reason why we don't expect school-age children to have the same sorts of temper tantrums that younger children do. A tantrum in a three-year-old is usually a reflection of that child's inability to use words to express the intensity of her emotions. Because those feelings are so overwhelming, they come out as kicks and screams. A seven-year-old, however, should have the verbal skills to share his emotions verbally instead of physically. That's why I'm more concerned when I see repeated temper tantrums in a school-age than child in a preschooler.

ious about staying overnight at a friend's house may express that concern indirectly, perhaps by talking about being afraid of bugs or burglars. No amount of reassurance that bugs won't harm him or that burglars can't get in will help.

The child's fear is symbolic, not literal. It is a way of testing the waters to see how his parents might respond to his underlying concerns. (Will he be abandoned, either figuratively or literally? Will his parents, who have been arguing more frequently recently, get a divorce while he's away? Will his younger sister, who's been ill, die if he's not there to protect her?)

Because of this symbolism, the list of things which children may say frighten them is endless. I've selected a few of the more common fears to show the underlying issues and how parents can approach them.

FEARS THAT FOLLOW VIOLENCE

In May 1988 an eight-year-old boy was shot to death in front of his classmates in a suburb of Chicago. A friend of mine, who is a child psychologist in that community, told me that she quickly started seeing the emotional fallout from the event. Five- and six-year-olds became afraid to leave their homes or to let their parents out of sight. One third-grade boy told his mother he would take a bazooka to school to protect himself. A ten-year-old talked incessantly about blood splattering on the floor. Even teenagers had trouble sleeping.

Few of these worried children attended the school where the shooting took place. Still, they were afraid—even if they did not or could not use words to describe their fears.

Children look to their parents to explain the unexplainable, be it a schoolroom shooting, an earthquake, a war, or a space shuttle explosion. Because they are so dependent on adults for their safety, the idea of random violence holds a special terror for children. It tears away the sense of order and predictability in their lives.

Parental understanding and empathy are especially important

when a safe haven, like a classroom, suddenly becomes dangerous. As with the suburban Chicago shooting, a child doesn't have to be directly involved to feel menaced.

This is why children can be deeply affected by the things they see on television. Helping children to cope with upsetting news reports and television programs requires parents to understand how children's minds work at different ages.

Part of the charm of children in kindergarten is the way they, like younger children, blur the line between fantasy and reality. We encourage young children, either openly or subtly, to believe that Big Bird not only exists, but can talk and roller-skate, too. To children this age, anything they see on television is real.

While older school-age children may understand that cartoon characters and superheroes don't really exist, they may still have trouble separating more subtle or complex fantasies from reality. This is especially true when they watch television or movies.

Research at Hunter College by Dr. Sherryl Browne Graves, who studies how children make sense of what they see on television, found that school-age children may have nightmares about television programs that didn't seem to frighten them at the time of viewing. This indicates that children process information differently from the way adults do. That means that if your children start having nightmares, you should think about what they might have watched on television or at the movies during the preceding week, not just during the previous day.

In addition, school-age children don't use the same coping mechanisms as adults do to handle threatening emotions. When an incident like the classroom shooting occurs, some adults who read or hear about it respond first with fear and then, as soon as they realize that their own children are safe in another school, with denial. We tell ourselves that such a thing couldn't happen in *our* neighborhood, or to *our* children. To admit that it might, and that our children are vulnerable, is too disturbing to face, at least for the moment.

Young children take a different approach: they "play out" the traumatic event. Usually that play occurs at home, with the children using toys or make-believe to work out their fears. Even young teenagers, whose play has largely shifted to organized sports, will often play games that re-enact the situations that have frightened them. Some older grade school children will write stories to help them come to terms with what has frightened them.

You can gain insights into how well your child is coping with his fears by watching how he plays. Make-believe that focuses on gory reenactments of the terrifying scene is not unusual, and can be very helpful—as long as the child controls the content, direction, and pace of the fantasy. Also, children's play and concerns may not focus on the overall event (the earthquake or plane crash), but on some small aspect, such as how their parents might find out if there were a fire or other emergency at school.

One sign of a problem, however, is if your child plays the same fantasy game over and over again. That lets you know that he isn't moving beyond his fears and concerns. He's stuck. If you can't help him get unstuck (perhaps by suggesting some different and happier endings for his fantasy play, or recommending that he add an ambulance or a police officer to his drawing of the disaster), he may require professional help.

Another sign that something may be wrong is if your child avoids talking about or playing through the frightening incident. Instead, his intense emotions may be expressed through physical symptoms such as sleeplessness or stomachaches. These psychosomatic problems can be subtle, especially in older children who have the verbal skills to "explain away" their problems. But if these symptoms last more than a week or two, a child should see a professional to help him handle his anxieties.

HELPING A CHILD HANDLE FRIGHTENING INFORMATION

To handle a terrifying and confusing incident, children take their emotional cues from the adults around them. That's why it's important for children to see that while their parents and teachers may be upset, they are coping with the situation and are aware of their own emotions.

In fact, your composure during a crisis is one of the best gifts you can give a frightened child. It allows her to "borrow" your emotional strength, and gives her a sense of security. By admitting at least some of your fears and concerns, and showing how you're responding to those emotions, you're teaching your child that her own fears can be overcome.

It's also important to remember that children who see something frightening always have three questions, even if they are unable to ask them directly: Am I safe? Are you (the people who care for me) safe? How will this affect my daily life? Only after those questions are answered will a child be able to put her images of a disaster into perspective.

Here are some other ideas and actions that can help when your child is frightened by real or imagined violence:

- You don't have to plunge right in. Remember that children this age often feel that, at some level, they are responsible for what has frightened them—even if this belief, from the parents' perspectives, is completely unwarranted and unrealistic. If you question children directly about their emotions, they may interpret what you say as a confirmation that what they are feeling or what they have done is somehow wrong. Their answers will be evasive.

  Instead of asking "Do you feel bad?" a better approach may be to say, "A lot of kids feel bad about this; do you?" This allows your child to feel safe talking about her scary emotions. You can also ask a child what she thinks her friends are feeling about the frightening event or situation. The description of her friend's emotions will usually mirror her own.

- Children in grade school may mention their concerns only obliquely, looking for hints as to why a tragedy occurred.

Preadolescents who have witnessed violence, for example, will often talk about the ways they might have predicted or prevented the tragedy.

It's important not to dismiss these comments as outlandish, but to view them as invitations to explore your child's feelings about herself and the incident. Let her know that you are open to talking about the situation whenever she wants to, even if she doesn't want to talk about it now.

- Don't be put off by a child's apparent bravado. I've seen bravado most often in boys who are in the third through sixth grade. Their talk will often focus on the things that frighten them the most, perhaps the blood and gore. Rather than tell a child this age not to talk about such things, recognize that this is a way for him to come to terms with his underlying emotions. Let him know that it's OK for him to have been and to still be frightened.

- Don't paint an inappropriately rosy picture of the situation by simply patting your child on the back and saying that everything will be fine. While such a message may come with the best of intentions, belittling the situation may hinder her ability to come to terms with her strong emotions. (It also denies the importance of her feelings.)

  Similarly, don't immediately rush in with reassurance if your child has a nightmare. Let her tell you about it while you hold her. Keep in mind that many children express their concerns symbolically rather than literally. If your child is frightened that she might lose her toys in a fire, don't be too quick to reassure her that they can be easily replaced. Those toys may represent her life as she has known it. It may frighten her to hear that you won't make an effort to save them.

- Be aware of what your children watch on television. Although children can be discriminating about books or movies, they often turn to television for companionship.

This means that children are increasingly likely to see violent or confusing images at the times they are most vulnerable—at night and when they are alone. If adults are not around, children may not get the reassurance and perspective they need to make sense of these programs.

• If you know about the collapse of a school building or a murder in your neighborhood that your child will probably learn about later in the news, talk to her about it first. She'll be less upset by information that comes from you, for she can ask questions and take her time understanding what happened. With an older child, you can explain to her that a local television news program, for example, might sensationalize a news event so that it sounds scarier and more dramatic than it was.[3]

• Recognize that news accounts and entertainment programs involving violence toward other children can be particularly disturbing. Children strongly identify with others their age. Stories about child abuse and neglect, schoolyard shootings, and suicide can both fascinate and confuse them. When they see another child threatened or hurt, they want to know it won't happen to them.

   Letting children know that a child who was abused or the victim of a crime wasn't a bad child can give them the permission they need to talk about their own concerns—even if those concerns are only tangentially related to the news story.

• Don't be afraid to talk to your child about accidents or violence. Ignoring an obviously frightening situation gives children the message that they shouldn't share what's on their minds because their thoughts and feelings might up-

---

[3] There's research evidence that both adults and children tend to overestimate the likelihood that they will be a victim of a violent crime. One reason for this appears to be the way violent crime is presented in the news media, especially on television. Newscasts' disproportionate emphasis on violence makes the world seem a much more frightening place than it actually is.

set you. This provides no outlet for a child's emotions and may make them all the more disturbing.

I remember how, when I was in elementary school, my mother and I would sometimes drive by the site of a car accident. Police officers would be directing traffic around the collision. Paramedics would be trying to help the victims. The scene would fascinate me. I'd want to watch.

My mother always told me to turn my head away. I couldn't understand why at the time. Besides, it only made me want all the more to look. What she was trying to do, of course, was protect me from seeing something upsetting. It never worked. But it did give me the message that she would be uncomfortable answering my questions about what had happened.

• Don't force information on your child. Parents sometimes overwhelm their child with more information than she can grasp at her age. Let your child's questions guide the depth and details of your answers. Always let her know that she can come back and ask you more when she's ready to do so.

COPING WITH A FAMILY CRISIS

Children can be profoundly affected by situations outside their daily experience. While they normally pay little attention to many aspects of the adult world, children become acutely sensitive to the emotional changes in their families when, for example, a parent loses a job or becomes ill. Their fears come not from the specifics of the situation, such as the economic downturn that triggered lay-offs or the prognosis of the illness, but from the disruption to the routine of their lives. Understanding this will help parents make more sense of their children's responses to a family crisis.

It's unusual to see these events—having a parent who loses a job and having a parent who becomes ill—lumped together when discussing child development. But there are at least two strong reasons to do so. First, there are remarkable similarities in how children respond to these events. Second, all too often they occur together, compounding the stress on parents and children alike.

Losing a job tests the mettle of a family. The emotional effects, felt by children and spouse alike, can be as severe as the financial consequences. The same can be said of the effects of a parent's medical problem.

One of the challenges faced by parents is to tell their children what has happened. It is a task many parents dread. Yet psychologists and others who work with these families say that their concerns about the children's reactions are often overblown.

The key is appropriate communication. A family crisis can actually improve the relationship between parents and their children. Parents who try to prevent their children from knowing what's going on will probably make matters worse. The children will sense the increased tension at home and, since no other explanation is available, will likely assume that they've done something wrong to cause it. In fact, the failure of the parents to admit that there's a problem may convince the children that they've done something horrendous.

That's why a child who hears from his mother that she's been upset because she has to find another job may feel more relieved than frightened. He now knows the source of the tension he has been sensing.[4]

---

[4] We can see clearly the potential negative effects of not telling a child what's going on in a case history shared by a psychologist I interviewed. The story is quite telling, even though it's about a slightly older child.

The psychologist had been consulted by a banker who was worried about changes in his fourteen-year-old daughter's behavior. The man had recently lost his job, but he was so concerned about his daughter's being upset that he told her very little about what was going on. He never mentioned to her that his severance package included a year's salary and that the family was in no immediate financial danger.

The girl assumed that his secretiveness meant that she wouldn't be able to attend college. She also assumed that this was such a touchy issue that she couldn't

Dr. Bruce Compas of the University of Vermont followed 125 families in which a parent had cancer. His research found that those parents who report good communication with their children about their illness said that the experience brought them closer together.

Once school-age children feel confident that they're not in any immediate danger and that you won't abandon them, they'll try to understand what losing a job or having a serious illness means. As with adults, they will use their personal frames of reference to get a handle on the situation. A child in the early grades may ask whether you lost your job or became ill because you did something bad—the adult equivalent of being sent to the principal's office for an offense committed at school.

This doesn't mean that young children will automatically have trouble coping with this new situation. Studies at the University of Vermont and at Sloan-Kettering Cancer Center in New York City have found that children under the age of ten have less difficulty than teenagers do in adjusting to having a parent diagnosed with cancer.[5] In fact, the things that may upset younger children the most are changes that they cannot understand and which haven't been explained to them, such as when a parent loses all her hair as the result of chemotherapy.

---

talk to him about it. In response—and without telling her parents—she switched her academic program at high school from the pre-college to the secretarial curriculum. She also started avoiding her old friends because she was embarrassed by what she saw as her family's plight.

The girl became depressed because she was concerned about her parents and didn't want to burden them with her fears. The parents became concerned because of the girl's depression.

[5] This may be due to one of the tasks associated with adolescent development. A crisis tends to draw family members closer together, both emotionally and through demands on everyone's time. Teenagers, however, are struggling to separate from their families and establish their independence. The family's need to pull together comes at a time when the adolescent is (and should be) focusing on herself. Because of this conflict, a teenager may feel angry, guilty, or depressed, but may not be able to talk about the underlying reasons.

SHARING THE BAD NEWS

There are several other things parents who have lost a job or become ill can do to help their children come to grips with the family's new situation:

- Tell your children, but don't feel you must rush in with the news. For example, most adults' first reactions to losing a job are shock, anger, and distress. The same holds true when they're diagnosed with an illness. It may take a few days or even a week to gain a better perspective on what this means for you and your family.

  If you talk to your child about it while you're still upset, she'll probably pay closer attention to the emotions in your voice than to your words. It's a good idea to wait until you've calmed down and worked out a plan for finding a new job before you broach the subject.

- Don't overwhelm children with information. Tell them enough to reassure them and to satisfy their curiosity, but not so much that they become confused and worried. Don't try to cover all the details in one talk. Most children do best processing what the situation means if they receive information in small doses, especially if they know they can come back and ask you questions.

  With younger children especially, focus your first talk on how this will effect their daily lives. Will you be spending more or less time at home while you're looking for a new job? Will you be going to the hospital for treatment?

- Maintain as many family rituals and routines as you can. You might not care or even notice if dinner's an hour later than usual, but your children may find it upsetting. Remember that young children in particular take comfort from the idea that the world is stable and predictable.

- Involve your children in planning some of your family's changes. This is especially important when it comes to daily or weekly routines, or if your lifestyle and finances will change dramatically.

  Suddenly telling your children that they won't be able to go to the movies or eat dinner out, if your family is used to doing those things, will leave them angry and perhaps worried. Instead, let them help you decide how the family will allocate the amount of money the adults decide can be used for entertainment. By being part of the decision-making process, children will feel more secure and empowered.

- Be sure your children know that they shouldn't feel ashamed. Remember that they may believe that you lost your job or became ill because you did something bad.

  It's very important that you let them know what they can tell their friends, so they don't feel they have to keep a family secret. In fact, it's a good idea for older children to talk to one or two of their close friends so that they don't feel isolated. Also, let them know that you're talking to your own close friends about the situation.

- Allow your children to help. Children are often eager to lend a hand, even though many of their efforts are more symbolic than practical. A young child can offer to share toys rather than request new ones. An older child might offer to take a cut in her allowance.

  It's important not to dismiss or belittle such offerings. They are a valiant and often appropriate attempt by the child to contribute to the family during a time of crisis, instead of seeing herself as a burden. Your children will feel good if they know that by cleaning their rooms or setting the dinner table, they're allowing you the time you need to focus on your job search or your health.

HOME ALONE — THE REALITY, NOT THE MOVIE

A psychologist acquaintance of mine once described to me a ten-year-old boy he had treated for a variety of anxiety-related problems. Apparently the boy would go directly from school to his empty apartment, where he would spend the three hours until his mother got home from work crouched behind the double-locked door, clutching his prize baseball bat in a death-grip and waiting for the dangerous intruder he feared would barge in at any moment.

Not all kids left home alone are so obviously fearful or express it so dramatically, of course. For many grade-school children, spending time alone at home is a source of pride. It is a confirmation that they are growing up and that their parents trust them. Being allowed to care for yourself after school or during an evening is an emotionally significant and memorable step toward adulthood.

For other children this age, however, time alone brings fear and depression. They feel abandoned by their parents, not empowered by them. The difference appears to stem both from the child's emotional readiness for the responsibility, and from the way the parents treat the situation.

National surveys conducted in the late 1980s found that between two million and six million children under the age of thirteen regularly cared for themselves without adult supervision after school or on weekends. For almost all parents of such latchkey children,[6] the decision to leave them alone is unwanted but unavoidable.

---

[6] The researchers often used the term "children in self-care." I prefer the more old-fashioned term "latchkey child," with its image of a boy or a girl wearing a key on a string around his or her neck so it won't be lost. One reason for my preference is that "children in self-care" sounds like it assumes the situation is

High-quality after-school programs in large cities, especially those for older school-age children, have not kept up with the demand. If they are not publicly financed, they can be prohibitively expensive. While there are proportionately more programs in the suburbs, transportation to and from them is often a problem.

The risks of allowing a child who isn't ready to be alone at home extend beyond the obvious household dangers of fires and injuries. One study conducted by Dr. Jean L. Richardson of the University of Southern California, which surveyed five thousand students in the eighth grade, found that those who were home alone for eleven or more hours per week were approximately twice as likely to use alcohol, tobacco, and marijuana as children the same age who spent all their time after school supervised by adults. The increased risk appeared no matter what the sex, race, or socioeconomic status of the children.[7]

So, when is a child old enough to spend time at home without adult supervision? While some states specify a legal age,[8] that does parents little good. According to research by Dr. Deborah Belle at Boston University, a child's chronological age doesn't tell a parent whether he's ready to spend time at home alone. Neither does the child's intelligence. While some of the children in her longitudinal study of fifty-three families handled staying home alone quite well, others couldn't motivate themselves to do their homework, or answered the door despite their parents' instructions not to do so. One child would forget to eat dinner unless an adult was there.

---

successful, that is, the child is caring for herself, when in many cases that's simply not true.

[7] The survey found that of the eighth graders who spent 11 or more hours per week trying to care for themselves, 23 percent had consumed more than 11 drinks of alcohol in their lifetime, 13 percent had smoked more than one pack of cigarettes, and 24 percent had tried marijuana. Among those who always had an adult caring for them at home, 11 percent had consumed more than 11 drinks of alcohol, 6 percent had smoked more than a pack of cigarettes, and 14 percent had tried marijuana.

[8] In New York, for example, leaving a child alone who's under the age of twelve constitutes child neglect. Of course, many parents hire baby-sitters who are younger than that. Usually the only time that law comes into play is when a young child is seriously injured while alone.

Children will often let their parents know when they are ready for the responsibility of staying at home alone. In fact, some can be quite insistent about it. Still, the best indicators of their readiness come from other behaviors. How well does she handle rules and responsibilities while you're around? Does she come home when she's supposed to? Does she do her homework without being prodded? Can she use kitchen appliances safely? Does she know what to do in case of a minor accident or an emergency?

If your child says she wants to forgo a baby-sitter for an afternoon or evening, it's a good idea to share those criteria with her. That will encourage her to show you how mature she is so that she can gain the privilege she wants. Keep in mind, however, that studies show that most children don't handle emergencies as well as their parents think they will. Just because an eleven-year-old can parrot back emergency instructions doesn't mean she'll remember those instructions during a crisis. Rather than simply asking your child to tell you what she would do if she cut herself badly or the stove caught fire, it's a good idea to have her act out those situations with you in as realistic a manner as possible.

CONQUERING FEARS OF BEING HOME ALONE

If you believe that your child is ready to spend time at home alone, there are several things you can do to help him feel more comfortable and confident in this new situation.

- Start with small separations. Even five or ten minutes alone in the house while you're in the front yard or at a neighbor's home isn't too small a first step for many children. This allows him to build his confidence and to avoid feeling overwhelmed.

  It's also a good idea to hold these first practice sessions and the first few separations during the day instead of at night. Shadows and unfamiliar sounds are much more frightening when it's dark outside. By gaining confidence during the daytime, a child will be much more comfortable with his first nighttime separations from you.

- Help your child identify the things that may frighten him. Remember that children (and adults, too, for that matter) are much more sensitive to creaky noises and other sounds when there's no one else around. Sit in the various rooms of your house with your child and listen for the sounds that the house makes. Help him identify such normally overlooked noises as the gurgling of the heating system and the hum of the refrigerator. That way your child won't be aware of those noises for the first time when he's alone. Also, go over how he should check whether the doors and the windows are locked.

- Allow your child to change his mind about staying at home alone. Some children who think they'll be fine alone discover that they become frightened or bored, and want to have an adult around the next time. When you return, talk to your child about his experience on his own. Make sure he knows that you really want to hear about any problems he's having—that you don't just want him to tell you that everything went well.

- Arrange for your child to call you or some other responsible adult, such as a grandparent or a neighbor, as soon as he arrives home, if you are not there. This ritual can make the transition to caring for himself less stressful for your child. Some research has shown that children who care for themselves most successfully appear to be those who sense they are still being supervised by adults. Another study by Dr. Deborah Belle of Boston University found that the more frequently children called their parents, the happier they were.

- In addition to providing your telephone number at work, prominently post at least one other number that he can call for reassurance during a scary moment or for nonemergency help. Many communities have telephone help services specifically for latchkey children who need an adult's guidance. Although some of the calls they receive are from children who want to know such things as whether they can let someone in the door, many are simple questions like "How do I turn on the toaster?" (It's a good idea to go over with your child ahead of time which appliances he can use, such as the toaster, the radio, and the television, and which he's not allowed to use, such as the stove and the microwave oven.)

- Agree on a schedule that tells your children what they can and should be doing when they get home from school. It's a good idea to work on this together, since that reinforces the trust you have in their maturity and self-reliance. Keep in mind that it's probably not a good idea to ask your child simply to do his homework until you arrive. There are several reasons for this. First, it makes homework an isolating experience. Second, that's probably not what your child would do at this time if you were home. While doing some homework is good, there should also be time to unwind, eat a snack, and do something that's fun.

- Give your child permission to enjoy himself. Being at home alone is a significant event for a grade-school child. He'll probably take his responsibility very seriously—especially if you emphasize all the things he shouldn't do while he's alone. Unfortunately, this one-sided approach tends to make children fearful. Remember to tell him what he can do that's fun.

5

Communication

If you must hold yourself up to your children as an object lesson (which is not necessary), hold yourself up as a warning and not as an example.
—GEORGE BERNARD SHAW (1856–1950)

That quotation from Shaw, which I certainly hope he said tongue-in-cheek, points to the complexity of parent-child interactions. All too often we think of our communication only in terms of words—the things we tell our children to do, the praise and consolation we offer in times of joy and disappointment, the warnings and the coaching.

Yet words are but one melodic line in the ongoing symphony of parent-child communication. How we each interpret that melody often depends on the underlying chords—our actions—which can add a dissonant or a supportive foundation to what we say.

This is seldom as simple as "Do as I say, not as I do!" or other such overworked phrases. School-age children are keen observers of the subtleties of adult behavior. We can see this not only in the habits they pick up—holding a fork the way Mom does, or affecting the same walk as Dad—but also in the ways they argue and negotiate with us.

By the time they're in the middle of elementary school, most children play a pretty good game of family politics. They're acutely aware of which parent is more likely to let them stay awake an additional half hour or give them an extra helping of dessert. They also know which strategies are likely to optimize their chances of getting what they want.

Such negotiating skill is a reflection of their ongoing cognitive and emotional development.[1] Their behavior offers us a window for observing how their brains are changing and how they perceive the world in new ways. By paying close attention, we can find reasons to be proud of and celebrate their growth—even when we're telling them they really do have to go to bed right now!

PLAYING ONE PARENT AGAINST THE OTHER

After his mother turned down his request to buy a particular item, a nine-year-old boy approached his father and asked if they might speak privately in the kitchen for a moment. The father, who realized what was going on, listened patiently to his son's request, and then asked him what his mother had said. "What's the matter?" the boy asked. "Can't you think for yourself?"

Children quickly learn the advantages of occasionally playing their parents against each other. By the time they're a few years old, they've realized that just because Mom has said no doesn't mean Dad won't say yes.

Toddlers and preschoolers view the world, including their parents, differently than older children do. They often see things in magical terms, as if simply asking for something is enough to make it appear. To children this age, parents are all-powerful. The ordinary constraints of time and money mean little to three-year-olds. When their requests are denied, our carefully crafted and logical

---

[1] I sometimes tell parents that all of the things that my son has done (so far) that have irritated, frustrated, or infuriated me are things that, from a developmental perspective, I wanted him to do. I just didn't want him to do them to *me* or at those particular moments!

explanations ("We can't drive that shiny car home because it belongs to someone else") offer them little comfort.

We can also see the egocentrism of preschoolers—that is, the firmly held belief that they are the center of the known universe²—in the way they try to play one parent off against the other. There is seldom any subtlety to their approach. In fact, if one parent says no to a request ("Can we keep a pony in our apartment?"), a four-year-old is likely simply to turn to the other parent and repeat the request using the same words.

A school-age child knows better. First, she's likely to anticipate some of her parents' objections. ("Can we *please* keep an Old English sheepdog in our apartment? I'll feed him and brush him and he won't be a bother to anyone. I promise!") Since even a seven-year-old knows that the sheepdog has a relatively low chance of being allowed to stay, the child will probably try to increase her odds by approaching each parent individually, and tailoring each request to that particular parent's personality, interest, and "soft spots." ("I have a way for you to save money on baby-sitters, Dad!")

While the request is unrealistic, the techniques she's using are actually quite sophisticated. They show her increasing ability to empathize with others. Instead of focusing only on her own emotions, she can more easily imagine how her parents might feel as well.

The elementary school years are also when children begin pitting one parent directly against the other, often when one of the parents is not around to set the record straight. For example, a child may try to convince his father that his mother gave him permission to watch a particular television program. Again, there is no malice or bad character in such attempts. They are simply a way for children to handle the people who have so much power over them.

While a certain amount of manipulation is normal and healthy,

---

² There's nothing wrong with thinking like this at that age. It's not a sign that the child is spoiled or selfish. Egocentrism is simply a reflection of the limits of a young child's cognitive and emotional development.

if it occurs constantly it may indicate underlying problems at home. Children who frequently pit one parent against the other may be acting out the tension they feel between their parents. That's one reason this type of manipulation is especially common among children whose parents are separated or divorced.

It can also be a problem in families where parents use children to apply emotional pressure on each other. For instance, instead of having family members openly discuss what they will do over a weekend, one parent may approach the children ahead of time about endorsing a particular plan. This sends a message that trying to manipulate people is acceptable.

It's important to remember that although they may not sound like it at the time, many children are reassured when they fail at testing their parents' resolve. Children get a feeling of security when they have predictable limits, even if they feel an obligation to test them every so often. In fact, the times when they make their most insistent tests may be the times when they need that reassurance the most.

SPECIAL PROBLEMS FOR DIVORCED PARENTS

A psychologist friend of mine told me of a recently divorced woman he was counseling. Her three- and nine-year-old children were driving her crazy by seemingly comparing her skills (and worth) as a parent to her ex-husband's. For example, when she would take the two children to a store, they would frequently ask for things that she could not afford. When she told them that, they would reply, "But Daddy would buy it for us!"

Here are some suggestions for handling these types of infuriating and demoralizing situations. While they're useful for all families, they're particularly important for stepfamilies and divorced parents:

- Remember that you seldom have to make a decision on the spot. If your child is asking for something you have reservations about, defer your decision until you've had a chance to think about it and discuss the matter with your spouse or ex-spouse. Let your children know that last-minute requests will be turned down. This way, they will be encouraged to give you more notice and discouraged from using time pressure to influence your decision.

- Set aside time to talk with your spouse or ex-spouse about rules. This can be quite difficult if your divorce was not amicable. But those are the families where agreements about the children are most important.

  You don't have to agree on everything, of course. But it's important to develop some informal guidelines. Remember that just because your spouse or ex-spouse supposedly lets your child go to bed an hour later doesn't mean that you must do the same thing. Children can adapt easily to houses that have different rules, as long as they know what those rules are. After all, the rules they must live by at school are quite different from those at home.

- Stepparents should usually defer to biological parents. Children in stepfamilies will often try to pit their biological parents and stepparents against each other as a way of testing the power structure of the new family. Power struggles between the stepparent and the child, in which seemingly trivial decisions may have tremendous symbolic value, can interfere with establishing a loving or even a respectful relationship.

  Discipline can be an especially thorny issue for stepparents. Children may act out or even taunt a stepparent as a way of seeing how that new relationship will change their lives. The stepparent—especially a stepfather in our culture—may feel an obligation to respond to such behavior by punishing the children.

But research by Dr. James H. Bray at the Baylor College of Medicine in Houston has found that, for the first few years at least, the family will do much better if discipline is left to the biological parent. This doesn't mean the children should be allowed to run wild. Rather, having the biological parent in charge of such issues prevents the children from driving a wedge between the parent and the new stepparent.

THE PRIVATE "I"

A friend of mine sounded upset when he described his five-year-old daughter's increasing desire to spend more time by herself. "When she's in a snit," he said, "she closes her door and tells us, 'Don't come into my room. I want to be alone.' "

He noted that the girl's increasing insistence on privacy didn't always cut both ways. She would usually respect her parents' wishes when they asked her to let them alone so they could work or spend time together. "But the bathroom is another matter," her father told me. "Frequently she'll come sashaying in when the door is closed."[3]

Privacy is a complex and confusing issue for children. The confusion stems from their conflicting needs for autonomy and acceptance. Asking for privacy is an opportunity for children to assert their growing independence and autonomy. At the same time, it is a rebuff to others that carries with it the risk of being rejected in return.

Children's concerns center on three areas: private time, privacy

---

[3] His complaint is far from unique. The mother of a boy that age told me how she was taking a shower one afternoon when her son led some of his friends from the neighborhood into the bathroom to ask if they could have some cookies. She figured the most diplomatic way of handling the situation was simply to agree so that they'd be motivated to leave quickly!

of feelings, and bodily privacy. The first signs of wanting to spend time alone seldom occur before children reach toddlerhood. Often children that age will quietly begin playing by themselves in an empty room, away from yet within earshot of their parents. Their behavior is, like so many things children that age try, a test of their independence.

The notion that thoughts and feelings can be private is a more sophisticated concept, which usually first appears a few years later. Children in preschool and kindergarten begin to understand that they have the ability to keep secrets. They play with this newfound power by whispering special messages to their friends and parents, for they now feel that they themselves can decide what others know about them.

By the time they reach kindergarten, bodily privacy usually becomes a concern, usually with a focus on nudity and using the bathroom. It is a reflection of their increased interest in sex differences and how their bodies work.

Recognizing when others may want privacy requires a level of empathy that only rarely develops before elementary school—even late elementary school for some children. Adults and adolescents recognize that if *they* want privacy, then others may want it as well. Younger children, with their natural egocentrism, approach the matter quite differently: I'm entitled to my privacy, and I'm also entitled to know what everyone around me is doing!

The desire for privacy can become profound toward the end of elementary school—especially for girls who have reached puberty ahead of their peers. These children may not understand why they suddenly feel like they want to be alone.

One reason may be hormonal, and reflects the onset of adolescent development. Another may be social, for privacy allows children to practice some of the soon-to-be-needed new skills that go along with dating and other new types of peer relationships. Privacy affords these children a chance to try new things without the fear of embarrassing themselves. Attempting a new hairstyle, rehearsing various ways of asking a classmate out on a date, writing a song—all are more easily and safely attempted away from the eyes and ears of others.

HANDLING PRIVACY PROBLEMS

Parents often feel ambivalent about their children's growing requests for privacy. On the one hand, it's a sign of the children's increased social and emotional maturity. On the other hand, it can be a painful barrier to communication.

We can see a child's growth in several areas by how he's likely to respond to the question, "What did you do in school today?" If you ask a four-year-old preschooler, he won't be able to give you a coherent answer. The problem isn't attitude, it's cognitive development. He simply doesn't yet have the skills to organize his experiences so that he can tell you extemporaneously how he spent his time. Yet if you ask him if they had story time, ate lunch, or sang songs, he's easily able to answer each of those questions.

A twelve-year-old will do a much better job of recalling and reciting his day. His brain has developed sufficiently that he can organize and prioritize his experiences—even if his priorities aren't the same as yours. But this is also an age at which it is common for children to begin to feel that their parents' questions are a bit intrusive.

Parents of preadolescents face a delicate balancing act as they try to stay aware of what their children are doing and feeling, remain open to their children's sometimes awkward or unclear requests for guidance and, at the same time, respect their privacy. It's important to remember that respecting a growing child's privacy doesn't mean losing touch with what is happening in that child's life.

In fact, not allowing a child enough privacy can foster some of the things that the parents are probably trying to prevent. Parents who are too intrusive can leave their children searching for new opportunities in which they have at least the illusion of exercising control, such as experimenting with drugs or sex.

Here are some things that can help strike the right balance between privacy and open communication:

- Talk about privacy as a privilege, not a right. As with all privileges, it comes with responsibilities. ("If you want to keep your room more private, then *you'll* have to make your own bed in the morning so that I don't have to come in as often.") Remind your children that even you have people—such as your employer and the Internal Revenue Service—checking whether you really did what you said you did.

- Make communication a two-way street. Remember that preadolescents are looking for a more balanced relationship with their parents that recognizes how they are maturing. The more you share your thoughts and feelings with your children, the more your children will do it with you.

  This doesn't mean you have to schedule formal "board meetings" with your kids. Often these exchanges are best done while puttering around the kitchen or watching a basketball game.

- Remember that preadolescents desperately want to talk to their parents or some other adults about the things they're doing and feeling. They just feel awkward and easily threatened—especially if you approach them with all the tact of a can opener cutting open a can of peaches.

  They'll share much more with you if you take an easygoing approach. Keep in mind that the first issue a child raises with you may not be what's really bothering or worrying her. It's often simply a way of testing the waters to see what sort of mood you're in and how judgmental you'll be.

  Restrain yourself from making quick comments, compliments, criticisms, and evaluations. Too early a response is often interpreted as insincere or intrusive. Instead, just listen and ask for clarification when necessary. Most important, pay full attention to your child when she's talking to you about her life.[4] If she senses you're not really listening, she'll stop sharing.

- Maintain family rituals, such as having dinner together, as a way of staying in touch with what everyone is doing and feeling. Children—including adolescents—thrive on this type of family predictability, even if they carp about it. It gives them a sense of belonging, and provides a feeling of stability while so much in their lives is changing.

- Look for ways to help your children get the privacy they need. This may be especially important if two or more of them share a bedroom. Some families set up a schedule of when siblings who share a room can have it to themselves. Encourage brothers and sisters to respect requests for privacy.

- Remember that your responsibilities as a parent are more important than your child's desire for privacy. It's important to respect your child's natural desire to keep some things to himself. But if you believe that your child is in trouble with drugs or the law, for example, you have an obligation to intervene.

  Signs of trouble include a significant drop in grades, a change in the types of friends with whom your child spends time, or the unexplained appearance of relatively expensive clothes or other possessions.

  If you feel you must check your child's room or check his mail, do so while he is there and explain why you're

---

[4] That doesn't mean you have to drop whatever you're doing and stare at her intently. In fact, focusing on her too much will probably make her feel self-conscious and reluctant to talk. There are advantages to having heart-to-heart talks while peeling potatoes. A good rule of thumb is that any activity during such important conversations should be relatively mindless. Your child knows that you can't read the newspaper and listen to her at the same time.

doing it. Talk about why you're concerned. That will help keep the conversation on the more important issues instead of just that of privacy.

FAMILY SECRETS

Family secrets can bind family members together or tear them apart. Being protected from the truth can breed a child's resentment and anger. So can knowing information that's inappropriate and emotionally overwhelming. Often, the contents of the secret are less important to the child than the way it is shared.[5]

By definition, a secret imposes a burden. It sets the information apart from other messages and, in a child's eyes, confers greater importance (and potential danger) to the topic. It also divides the child's family or community into those who share the secret and those who do not, decreasing trust and stifling communication in areas unrelated to the secret.

There's also an irony to asking children to maintain a shameful family secret. The request itself perpetuates the shame and encourages the children to feel ashamed of something that is out of their control and, consequently, to feel ashamed of themselves.

For your children, the content of a secret may be beyond their ability to understand and put into perspective—a combination that often increases fears. For example, telling a seven-year-old that you may have to file for bankruptcy, but that she shouldn't tell her friends or the neighbors, will do little except raise her anxieties.

---

[5] Let me give you an example. A psychologist colleague of mine once told me that her parents shared a secret with her on her eighteenth birthday: her mother was dying of cancer. The parents' justification for not telling her earlier had been that they didn't want to upset her. In reality, however, my friend had spent the previous five years upset and confused because she didn't understand why her mother, who obviously was ill, wasn't getting any better. Instead of feeling protected, she felt betrayed. The memory of the incident also adds a touch of bitterness to her birthday every year.

Although the words do not mean much to her, she can sense the tensions in the household. She may worry that she's the cause of the problem (why else would it be a secret?), and fantasize about its dire consequences.

In that situation, the adults in the family will tend to focus their interests on the financial details. School-age children, however, will be more concerned with fundamental issues, such as whether they'll still be able to live in the same house and eat dinner every night.

While children will seldom raise such issues directly, they may need reassurance that they won't be abandoned by their parents. Such reassurance is especially important during family crises, like a pending divorce or a family member's illness. Keeping the situation a total mystery will confuse children and lead them to develop their own theories to explain their family's unusual behavior. But telling children too much can also confuse them, especially if they're asked to keep that information to themselves.

Discussing a family crisis is, perhaps, analogous to sex education. You need to share information with your children, but only as much as they can understand and need to know at their age.

Children in single-parent families may be more likely to be asked to keep inappropriate secrets. The parent may fall into the trap of treating the children more like adults, and may tell them information that puts those children in an emotional bind. This is especially true for children whose parents are divorced. Dad may ask that they not tell Mom about his girlfriend, or Mom may request the same about her boyfriend.

Children should never be asked to keep such a secret, because it puts them in an untenable position. If they keep one parent's secret, they are betraying the parent they don't tell. If they share the secret, they are being disloyal to the parent who told them. From their point of view, they can't win, no matter how they behave. It is the children, not the parents, who suffer from such secrecy.

G O O D S E C R E T S A N D B A D S E C R E T S

There are some shared secrets that seem to help children feel better about themselves. Learning the truth about Santa Claus, for example, appears to make children feel more mature, especially if there's still a younger child in the family who doesn't know. Other secrets are clearly destructive, despite the best intentions of the parents in keeping or sharing them.

Here are some things to keep in mind when deciding whether to share a family secret with your children:

- In general, don't tell your children anything you don't want them to share. Young children in particular feel an internal emotional pressure to share secrets. In fact, telling a child in kindergarten or early elementary school to keep some information to herself may make her more likely to talk about it because of its greater perceived value. That's one reason children will quickly offer to share a secret: as a proof of friendship.

  The secrets you share with children in early elementary school should be short-term and innocuous, such as a birthday surprise for a family member. That way they get to share the fun, and there's minimal risk.

- Ask yourself if the information has any direct bearing on your children's lives. If Uncle Joe in Minneapolis, whom they barely know, is having an affair or has lost his job, there's no need to tell your children, because it doesn't affect them directly. (It's also, quite frankly, none of their business.) But if their beloved grandmother's health is failing, you shouldn't hide it from them.

  Use this guideline, as well as your children's ages, to determine which aspects of the information you should share with them. Although they may not understand their grandmother's illness, they will probably want to know whether she's in pain or why she doesn't recognize them.

- Answer your children's unasked questions. Remember that during any family crisis, children have three questions that their parents should address, even if the children don't ask them directly: Will I be all right? Will you (the important people in my life) be all right? How will this affect my daily life?

  By answering these questions first, parents will help their children keep any other information they're told about the crisis in better perspective.

ANGER AT YOUR CHILD

Anger—no, fury—is among the "dirty little secrets" of parenthood. I hear this anger all the time when I give speeches and workshops to parents. It's simmering beneath the surface—the unasked question behind the innocuous one. Much of that anger is centered on parent-child communication.

While parents talk about and glorify their feelings of love and protectiveness, their normal and often predictable moments of rage toward their children are seldom brought into the open. It is as if acknowledging the intensity of their anger is an admission of inadequacy or failure. If we deny it, perhaps it will go away, or we can convince ourselves that it never happened at all.

But a child's ability to bring out anger in his parents is usually a sign of normal development. A toddler who is testing the limits of her independence will reject her parents occasionally, ignoring their pleas that she not spill the apple juice on the rug. A ten-year-old will leave his room a mess and a fifteen-year-old will shave half his head as ways of declaring that they are no longer under their parents' control. These children may view the anger they see bubbling up in their parents as a confirmation that they have been successful at pushing the envelope of social acceptability.

The conflicts that trigger the most intense responses often tell us more about ourselves than about our children. Our most dramatic reactions to our children's behavior often come when we're feeling hurt. The child most likely to set off that strong, emotional response is the one who is most like us—especially when that child reminds us of things we don't particularly like about ourselves.[6]

This emotional volatility is compounded by pressures at home or at work that have nothing to do with the parent-child relationship. It's at these times that we become disproportionately upset at our children over trivial incidents. Even anger at a spouse or boss is sometimes acted out on the children. Financial problems can trigger rage at a child's innocent request for a toy.

How we handle that anger (whether justified or not) is more important than the anger itself. Some parents feel swept away by it, as if the anger is a direct result of their children's behavior, and not within their own control. They feel manipulated by their children and, at the same time, upset by their own feelings of help-lessness. (The feeling that you're out of control is a red flag that you should be taking another approach. Family counseling is one good way of getting the outside perspective that you need.)

Other parents show their need to control their children by imposing strict rules. But if those rules aren't flexible enough to match the child's changing needs and development, they'll backfire. Children from overcontrolled homes learn that the way to get attention from their parents is to be passive. For example, if they don't do their homework, their parents are likely to become frantic.

From a child's perspective, such behavior is simply a way of exercising power. Parents can't force a child to study. The more adults push the schoolwork, the more passive (and powerful) the child becomes. The parent's feelings of anger accentuate the loss of control over the child's life.

One way to handle such situations is to choose your battles care-

---

[6] There are exceptions to this, of course. One of the most obvious is when a divorced parent sees images of his or her ex-spouse in the child—a perception that is usually unfair, even if technically accurate.

fully. By giving the child more control over the minor issues (e.g., how neat his room is or what clothes he wears to school), he'll have the power and recognition he craves, and will be more likely to go along with the two or three things that are really important to you.

Another useful approach is to pair new privileges with new but related responsibilities. ("If you want to play Little League baseball in your team uniform, you'll have to put it in the laundry hamper after each game.")

The growing verbal skills of school-age children mean that many of the behaviors that are likely to upset parents are verbal. We treasure our children's use of language, until they use what they've learned to talk back. Phrases like "Who cares?" and "You can't make me!" suddenly start cropping up in what, months or years earlier, would have been more polite conversations.

Parents are often too quick to interpret this behavior as disrespectful, when it may simply be a reflection of a child's normal development. In fact, a child who never talks back may be at higher risk for getting into serious trouble later on than one who does.

When you think about it, you'll realize that we often give children confusing and even contradictory messages about what they say. We don't want them to automatically go along with what their friends say, so we tell them not to cave in to social pressure. Yet the behavior that we call "standing up for yourself" when addressed toward a classmate is labeled "talking back" when it occurs to a parent or teacher.

All children are impudent and sassy at times. Yet they may view the situation and their behavior quite differently than their parents do. A two-year-old will often say "No!" as a way of finding out what reaction it will provoke from his parents. A preschooler may simply be mimicking the style of communication he hears at home and assumes to be appropriate.

While some young children copy their parents' behavior, others are inspired to talk back by what they hear from characters on television. Since rude, sassy behavior on television comedies is often accompanied by laughter and cheers, children may get the idea that it's not only acceptable, it's funny.

Talking back can be a particular problem for parents of intelligent, articulate school-age children because their verbal skills may have outpaced their social skills. A verbally precocious child may not yet have the empathy and diplomacy he needs to raise an issue or express his desires without appearing to challenge his parents.

What the parents may view as back talk, the child may see as an opportunity to practice negotiating skills. A six-year-old who wants to strike a bargain at the dinner table that he gets an extra cookie if he eats three more string beans is experimenting with the limits of his power and new ways of getting his parents' attention. As he grows older, he learns that words are not always necessary. He can provoke his parents (and thereby show his power) with a carefully timed look of disgust or a raised eyebrow.

A sudden increase in back talk can also be a sign of a deeper problem that the child feels uncomfortable expressing directly. If parents are having difficulty with their marriage, a child may talk back as a way of distracting them from the adult arguments that are making her nervous. An only child whose mother becomes pregnant may suddenly talk rudely to both parents. She can't think of other ways to get the extra attention she craves, so she does what she's sure will provoke a reaction.

HANDLING THE ANGER

It is, perhaps, paradoxical that the intensity of a parent's fury at a child is a sign of their closeness. Our children elicit such dramatic responses because they have been studying us more intensely than anyone else ever has. They know exactly which emotional buttons to push to spur us into action—or at least guarantee a response.

Still, repeated and destructive anger toward your child can lead to serious problems. Here are some things to keep in mind:

- Pay close attention to your own emotional state before talking to your child about emotionally sensitive subjects. All too often, we feel pressure as parents to handle situations as soon as they arise. But if you're feeling tired, has-sled, or frustrated, that's not a good time to talk to your child about the D on her report card.

- Look for ways to release pressure that's building up in your family. It's a good idea to hold a family meeting oc-casionally to discuss whether everyone's expectations of each other are realistic and appropriate. Children who participate in decisions about their responsibilities are less likely to rebel against them.

  If your family's overstressed and overscheduled, you have to build in some "downtime." That doesn't have to be as elaborate as a two-week trip to the Bahamas.[7] It can be a weekly ritual of watching your family's favorite television show together.

- When you're angry, focus your emotions on your child's behavior, not on your child. Avoid character assassination or doom-and-gloom predictions about how they'll never make anything of themselves. Such broad statements are not only ineffective and inappropriate, but they're likely to backfire.

  If you're angry at your child's behavior, she'll know what she has to change. If you're angry at her as a per-son, she'll simply become defensive and get angry back at you. For example, if your child accidentally spills her juice on the living room carpet while rushing through the room, don't tell her that she's clumsy. She already knows she made a mistake. Instead, remind her that she shouldn't run with a drink in her hand.

  You should also insist that she help clean up the spill. This is important for two reasons. First, it's the polite and appropriate thing for her to do. Second, it helps her

---

[7] In fact, some adults find such vacations both stressful and disappointing. It is the paradox of the drive that may make them so successful at work. They treat their relaxation as yet another goal to be accomplished: "We're going to relax and have fun together—or else!"

"wipe the slate clean" by taking responsibility for the
mess she caused, and allows her to stop feeling guilty or
upset about it.

- Be sensitive to what you teach your children by your actions as well as by your words. Parents (myself included)
fall into this trap all the time, such as by yelling at a child
to be quiet or telling a child in public that she shouldn't
say things that embarrass other people. Ideally, when
you're angry you should act in a way that shows your
child how you'd like her to handle her own anger
toward you.

- No matter how tempting it is, don't respond to an apparently defiant child in kind. Answering with something like
"Don't talk back to me!" gives the child control of the
situation and is likely to escalate the behavior. It also
demonstrates an inappropriate way for your child to in-
teract with a family member.

  Instead, let the child know that she's hurt your feelings, and why.[8] That usually stops the behavior, and at
the same time lets her know you've heard her. If that
doesn't work, try switching roles: let her know what she
sounds like.

- Look for patterns to the back talk. Does it happen only
at home or at school? Most back talk occurs at home because children feel safer expressing strong emotions there.
They know that they are less likely to be seriously hurt or
permanently rejected by family members than by others.

------

[8] I remember some family members, who shall remain nameless, who used this
approach in the hope of instilling guilt rather than insight in their children. What
they eventually stirred up was resentment instead.

   If you use this technique, try to be matter-of-fact, not melodramatic. Your child
simply may not realize that the words she is using are upsetting or painful to you.
Even if she does, by letting her know how and why they bother you, you're treating
her in a way that recognizes her growing maturity. That by itself may be enough
to get her to stop.

That's why they may verbally strike out at a parent or sibling even though the underlying problem—the issue that really needs to be addressed—has to do with a classmate at school or a neighbor.

Also, ask yourself if it's happening with all adults or only with parents. If your child is talking back to everyone, you should get her some professional help.

• Think about whether your child is simply looking for extra attention. Remember that children often prefer to have you yelling at them than ignoring them. It's a sign of how important you are in their lives.

Also, look for things in your family life that may be upsetting your child, such as a forthcoming move to a new house or an ill grandparent. The back talk may be a way for your child to release the tension she's feeling about those types of issues. If that's the case, talking about what's really troubling your child will stop the problem behavior.

6

Discipline

It is better to bind your children to you by a feeling of respect, and by gentleness, than by fear.
—TERENCE (185–159 B.C.), *Adelphi*

There's a common misconception I encounter wherever I give lectures or workshops both to parents and to professionals: the belief that discipline and punishment are the same thing. That's simply not true. The word *discipline* shares the same Latin root as the word *disciple*. It has to do with teaching. Whenever you discipline a child, you should ask yourself what you're teaching that child.

Many of these teachings come from your actions much more than your words. Haim Ginott, a psychologist who had both wonderful insights into parent-child interaction and a keen eye for irony, used to describe a six-foot-tall father bending over to swat his kindergarten-age son so that the boy would learn to "pick on someone his own size." As is so often the case, the message in the parent's behavior was antithetical to what the parent had wanted.

There are definite techniques for disciplining children effectively, such as positive reinforcement, time out, and the occasional sincere threat. (Children know you're not serious when you tell them that they'll be grounded for the next twenty-five years, but they'll pay very close attention if you mention not being able to watch television for three days!) Still, discipline is much more an art than a science. In many ways it resembles an improvised dance, in which each dancer responds to the movements of the other, playing off each other's strengths and weaknesses, needs and desires.

Discipline for school-age children is different from that for infants, toddlers, or preschoolers, because of the dramatic growth and increased sophistication of their brains. They are better able to think abstractly, and can therefore see alternatives to their behaviors that younger children could not imagine.

If you ask a preschooler to clean up his toys, for example, he may simply pile them in the middle of the room. But a school-age child can understand that the goals of cleaning up toys include not just clearing a path on the floor, but being able to find those toys later on. Discipline for these older children should include helping them think about and understand the consequences of their behaviors, such as not having to search all over the house for a favorite toy.

I've written in earlier books about spanking and other forms of corporal punishment as discipline techniques.[1] Aside from any philosophical or moral stands on corporal punishment of children, I'm against it for very practical reasons: research has shown it not only to be ineffective, but often to be counterproductive. This is especially true when spanking and the like are the sole or primary forms of discipline used by parents. While spanking may seem to be effective in the short term, it quickly loses its power to influence a child's behavior. Besides, repeated corporal punishment teaches young children that it's appropriate for strong people to control weaker and smaller people with physical violence. Ask yourself: Is that really the sort of thing you'd like your child to grow up believing?[2]

---

[1] *Parent & Child: Getting Through to Each Other* (New York: William Morrow & Company, 1991); *Toddlers and Preschoolers* (New York: William Morrow & Company, 1994).

[2] A few years ago I received a mailing promoting a book written by two psychologists that promised techniques to make any child instantly and permanently obedient. Upon closer examination, the authors were advocating little more than having parents bully and intimidate their children—something that's quite easy to

I'm always amazed at parents who tell me things like, "We keep spanking him, Doc, but he just keeps acting that way!" I ask them why, if the spanking isn't working, they keep doing it. The answer almost always is that they can't think of anything else to do—often because spanking is how their own parents tried to discipline them when they were children. What they need is skill at using other techniques that are more effective and less likely to backfire.

Having said that, I must mention that one or two swats on the backside over the course of your child's development won't permanently warp his psyche. (They probably won't change his behavior much, either.) But if you ever feel that you *must* hit your child to control him, you should look for some outside help such as family counseling. The problems that trigger that feeling are seldom only your child's behavior.

REWARDS VERSUS BRIBES

All parents resort to bribing their children at some point. It's usually a last-ditch effort aimed at quieting a five-year-old who's whining loudly in the supermarket checkout line or at controlling a ten-year-old on the brink of a social disaster. The promise of a pizza, a toy, or a few extra dollars can have dramatic, if temporary, effects on a child's behavior.[3]

do with a three-year-old, but much more problematic with a teenager.

When I read the promotional material, my mind flashed back to a graduate course I'd taken which dealt, in part, with the social structure of wolf packs in the wild. In each pack there's a dominant male wolf, known as the alpha wolf, who maintains his leadership by threatening and beating up the other males who challenge him. Eventually, however, one of the other wolves grows big enough, strong enough, and daring enough to beat up the alpha wolf and become the pack's new leader. This younger wolf, too, maintains his position by repeating the cycle of growling and fighting until another wolf takes him down. Was this what those authors wanted to see in their own families?

[3] Not all the time, of course. In one of my *New York Times* columns I wrote about a couple whose son wasn't getting good grades in junior high school. His parents had tried everything from hiring tutors to lecturing him about how impor-

But what happens if bribery becomes the main technique parents use? Is a little bribery such a bad thing? While bribes often do produce a high degree of effort from children, they can have negative long-term effects. Those problems are most likely to occur when a child is repeatedly bribed and comes to depend on bribes, even for ordinary tasks.

Small external rewards, like a shiny sticker, a piece of candy, or a few complimentary words, are powerful incentives for young children. The reward helps them focus their efforts on a task until they can see and feel for themselves the benefits of what they have done. A five-year-old, for example, may not understand the value of cleaning her room or of washing her hands before dinner. A new dinosaur sticker for her collection or some extra attention provides enough of a reward until she grows older and has stronger internal motivations.

One problem with bribery is that instead of acting as a transition to these internal motivations, it can become the primary focus of the child's efforts. The natural rewards that come with doing a job well or being part of a group are overshadowed and go unnoticed, making it less likely that the child will do the job again without another bribe.

In addition, any behavior associated with a bribe can immediately become suspect in children's eyes. They reason, sometimes with great accuracy, that if their parents offer them something expensive or unusual for trying a new food, for example, it must really taste bad. While routine chores, such as clearing the table or washing the dishes may not be very interesting activities, children can enjoy the feeling they get that they are helping to make their

---

tant his school records would be for the rest of his life, all to no avail.

Finally they decided to bribe him. They gave him a credit card. It was, predictably, a major disaster. Not only did the boy spend several hundred dollars a week on things for himself and his friends, but his grades were still bad.

There are several reasons why this approach was doomed from the start. The use of the credit card was not contingent upon his studying and other behaviors the parents hoped for. The card didn't meet the boy's pressing emotional needs— needs which he tried to address by buying things for his friends. But what's particularly striking was how out-of-proportion and inappropriate giving a credit card to a young adolescent is, in any circumstances, even as a blatant bribe.

family work. If parents offer a bribe for performing basic tasks, that makes those chores appear much less attractive.

So telling a child who dislikes arithmetic that you will give him $20 for finishing his math homework—which is clearly a bribe, since he should be doing it anyway—is likely to backfire by making the arithmetic even less attractive than it already is. At the same time, offering a bribe can make your child see the bribe itself as less valuable or enticing than it otherwise would be. In other words, the child figures that if you're offering her a pizza if she cleans up her room, that pizza can't be very good.

An occasional bribe, whether in response to a crisis or simply at a time when you want a little peace and quiet, probably won't lead to large problems later on. Keep in mind, however, that you want your child eventually to be motivated and rewarded by the tasks themselves. You should offer the smallest reward necessary to get the job done.

BREAKING THE BRIBERY HABIT

A child who has been repeatedly bribed will tend to up the ante for every request a parent makes. Here are some things you can do to avoid that problem, or to break the cycle if you feel you've been bribing your children too much:

- Let your child know that you are aware of and respect her opinions. After all, no one really enjoys taking out the garbage. By stating that you realize it is sometimes a smelly and messy job, you are letting her know that her feelings are valid, but that she must still do her part. If you try to convince your child that something is interesting or fun when it isn't, you're telling her that her feelings don't count. You're also lying—and she knows it.

   The same holds true for doing homework. Acknowledge that sometimes it isn't fun and that it might be more pleasant to talk on the telephone or watch television; but make it clear that this doesn't mean she can avoid her

school assignments. Taking this approach avoids your being sidetracked into name-calling and battles over whether
your child is lazy.

• Focus your attention on your child's behavior instead of
the results or the reward. That helps with the transition
to the child's own internal motivation and sense of accomplishment. If you're concerned about your child's
grades, for example, praise her or offer other small rewards for daily studying—the behavior you really want
and that your child can control—instead of waiting for
report cards. If you put more emphasis on conveying a
sense of appreciation for your child's behavior than on
the reward, your child is less likely to become dependent
on the reward.

Also, involve your child in figuring out a study schedule. That makes her more likely to follow through than if
you simply imposed some new rules.

• Remember how tremendously reinforcing some extra attention from you is for your children. Parents sometimes
feel they have to use more and more expensive rewards,
when what their children really want them to do is spend
more time with them.

• If you want to break the cycle of bribery, do it dramatically. Hold a family meeting. Announce that there are going to be some significant changes.

Be very clear and explicit about the new rules. Explain what behaviors are expected of your children simply
because they're members of the family. These might include such things as doing their schoolwork, helping set
the dinner table, and putting their dirty laundry in the
hamper. Explain—firmly—that there will be no more
bribes. Also, go over the consequences of not doing
what's expected of them. ("If you don't do your homework, you won't be allowed to watch television or play
video games. If you don't put your dirty clothes in the

hamper, they won't be washed.") Remember that most
children will, within a day or two, challenge those new
rules to see if you were serious about change. Be prepared.

Apologize to your children for having bribed them.
Don't get hung up on your own guilt. Instead, be glad
you realized what was happening, and move on.

DAMNING WITH FEIGNED PRAISE

I mentioned earlier that praise from adults is a very strong moti-
vator for children. It boosts their self-esteem and increases the likelihood that they will repeat whatever behavior brought about the
praise. Yet research has shown that the relationships between
praise, self-esteem, and behavior are not as simple as once thought.
Excessive praise for a mediocre performance can be more disturbing to a child than having that performance ignored. The most
effective praise is sincere, credible, and spontaneous.

Children who receive too much inappropriate or undeserved
praise from their parents tend to become less concerned with how
well they do tasks and more concerned with how other people
evaluate them. For example, they may be more interested in the
grades they receive than with learning new and useful things at
school.

School-age children are pretty good at spotting and devaluing
inappropriate praise. Teachers, unfortunately, don't always recognize this, and may do unintended damage by effusively praising
a child for mediocre performance.

Dr. Sandra Graham, an educational psychologist at the University of California at Los Angeles, ran an experiment in which
she showed school-age children videotapes of two children solving
arithmetic problems. One child was praised highly for doing the
work. The other was simply told he did a good job. When she

asked the children watching the tape which arithmetic student was less smart, most said it was the one who got all the praise. They interpreted the teacher's behavior as a sign that she didn't think as highly of that child.

The incidents from my own childhood that clearly supported this interpretation had more to do with sports than with academics. The poorest player on a Little League or camp baseball team— the one who swung at and consistently missed the ball all season long—would often be praised effusively by the coach if he hit a foul ball or a pop fly that was caught.

But even this child knew that the better players were only told that they made a nice effort in those situations, or that it was just some bad luck. By paying special and inappropriate attention to what the child knows is a failure, the coach unintentionally reinforced how different the poor player was from the other, more competent children on the team.

KEYS TO EFFECTIVE PRAISE

To make the most of any praise you offer to a child, keep the following things in mind:

- Focus your praise on the child's specific actions and efforts, such as studying for a test or practicing the piano. If you are specific about what you are praising and recognize the accomplishment, the child will learn to judge a good performance and will be likelier to be motivated to keep doing a good job.[4]

---

[4] In my book *Toddlers and Preschoolers* (New York: William Morrow & Company, 1994) I cited some research by Dr. Michael Lewis of the Robert Wood Johnson Medical School. The research had brought to light a disturbing tendency of the parents of young girls to use praise differently than the parents of young boys. The parents of boys tended to be specific and focus their praise on behaviors ("You did such a good job of building that tower out of blocks!"). When girls did the same thing, however, the parents tended to use praise in broader, nonspecific ways ("Oh, you're such a smart girl!").

The boys, because of the specificity of the praise, learned how to judge for

Problems sometimes arise when a parent glosses over the work that the child did. For example, when a child gets an "A" on a test, some parents will praise the child by saying, "I always knew you were smart!"

Unfortunately, that type of praise can become a burden to a child because it attributes the accomplishment to her innate ability instead of to her effort. She may now feel that she has to prove that she's not so smart so that she can rid herself of that burden.

• Be selective in your praise. As described above, children often interpret unwarranted praise as a put-down. If you praise everything your child does, she will become anxious about whether she'll continue to get your praise.

• Adjust your expectations to your child's level of development. While a toddler deserves praise for naming an object or eating with a spoon, the same praise is inappropriate for a kindergartner. A child that age has already mastered those simple tasks and will be more encouraged by praise that focuses on new challenges.

It's usually very easy to tell when a preschooler or young school-age child is proud of an accomplishment, even when she can't put her feelings into words. She'll hold her head erect, smile, and puff out her chest when she succeeds at something that's really challenging. But when she succeeds at an easy task, she won't show this obvious and contagious pride.

• Pay attention to how you give praise to other family members. One of the first things to disappear in marriages that are in trouble is the skill of noticing everyday behaviors that deserve a positive comment. It's important that parents compliment each other appropriately in front

---

themselves the quality of their work. The girls, who received repeated but more global praise, had more difficulty judging their accomplishments and were more dependent on the opinions of others to determine how well they'd done.

of their children. That demonstrates an important way of showing that you care about someone and makes for a more pleasant home too.

ARGUMENTS AS A SIGN OF GROWTH

Family conversations sometimes take on the intensity and strategies of a tennis match at Wimbledon. The child serves his request, has it stopped at the net by the parent, then tenaciously responds with different verbal shots, trying to score his point.

"May I stay up another half hour?" "No." *"Why not?"* "It's your bedtime." *"But everyone else stays up later!"* "Go to bed." *"Please, just this once."* "That's what you said last time." *"How about another twenty minutes?"* "Ten minutes." *"But . . ."* "Ten minutes, and not a second more!" *"Oh, OK."*

Game, set, match.

While it's easy to read malice into children's manipulations, this is seldom the case. Rather, these arguments are a sign of children's growing abilities to think abstractly and to use words. They show how sensitive children are to their parents' emotions, for children quickly learn which ploys are most effective at getting what they want from each of the important adults in their lives.

These verbal sparring matches are also a reflection of the messages we give children in other situations: that they should stand up for themselves, stick to a task, and not give up easily. Although it may not feel like it at the time, we should be proud of our children when they attempt these types of negotiations.

These parent-child interactions serve another important purpose. They allow children to test how stable and predictable the rules that govern their lives are. The overall tone of these disagreements and negotiations reflects how the parents have handled similar situations with their children in the past.

One sign of a problem is if you repeatedly have to say no to the same request. The tip-off here isn't the word itself, but its rep-etition. If you have to say no several times, that means your child recognizes that in the past a series of noes sometimes leads to a yes. The early noes have no meaning or power.

From the child's perspective, repeatedly asking for something that has already been denied is like playing a slot machine in Las Vegas. Sure, he loses most of the time, but every so often he wins a jackpot. It's that occasional reinforcement that keeps the child plugging away at his parents.

In fact, it's the occasional nature of the rewards (known as a variable-ratio reinforcement schedule) that makes this pattern so difficult to break, and children so tenacious in their attempts to change your mind. Also remember that, unlike gamblers in a ca-sino, your children seldom have anything to lose by repeating their requests.

What adults often interpret as verbal baiting by children can have other meanings as well. When pressed, children will do something that makes their parents furious as a way of simply getting attention from them. From the children's perspective, even getting yelled at is better than being ignored. That shows how much they value any attention they receive from their parents.

Sometimes children who have had a difficult day at school will bait their parents as a way of exercising some power in their lives. A child who feels he has little or no influence over his parents will sometimes deliberately do something to make them angry. But his goal is not to upset them; it's to prove to himself and his parents that he still has some power, even if it's only the power to annoy.

School-age children may also appear verbally aggressive when they're trying to figure out the appropriate social contexts for dif-ferent behaviors. They often have not learned that the language and behaviors that seem to work well with their peers on the street or the playground generate different responses from their family. Although parents may interpret such behaviors as manipulative or unloving, the children are simply behaving in ways that are normal or even adaptive in the neighborhood or at school, where an as-sertive or aggressive child gets the teacher's attention.

STRATEGIES FOR CHANGING BEHAVIOR

It doesn't help simply to punish a child for whining, talking back, or doggedly begging for something he has already been denied. In fact, yelling at your child for yelling at you will probably do more harm than good since your actions contradict your words. Your child needs to know what types of behaviors you find acceptable, even if they don't guarantee his satisfaction. Here are some ideas that can help:

- Try changing roles. It's important to do this with respect, not mockery, if your child is going to learn from the experience. Let your child hear what his different styles sound like to you. ("Put yourself in my position for a minute. Tell me how you'd feel if I said this to you." You repeat, as accurately in tone as you can, what your child said. "Does that sound like a good way to get me to do something? Let's try to figure out what might be a better way.")

  Be sure you also let him know what being reasonable and respectful sounds like. That way he has behaviors he can emulate instead of simply hearing which one he should avoid, but not knowing the alternatives.

- Pay extra attention to your child when she acts the way you wish. Parents often fall into the trap of ignoring their children's good behavior and getting upset with them when they behave badly. Children quickly learn that misbehaving will get them the extra attention they crave. If you pay attention to a child who is acting and speaking politely, you will increase the likelihood that she will be polite the next time she wants something from you or anyone else.

- Let your child suffer the natural consequences of his behavior. I'm assuming that those consequences aren't dangerous or painful, of course.[5] For example, some children repeatedly ignore their parents' announcements that supper is ready. They have learned that the only thing that happens when they ignore the call to come down to a meal is that another call comes a minute later.

Instead, simply start eating your meal without them. Not getting their favorite piece of chicken, eating cold food, or missing a meal completely won't do them any real harm. It will, however, teach them to pay closer attention to what you say the next time you call them.

• Let your children know that you recognize their growth and development. Often, children will repeatedly ask for an object or a privilege an older child has received. Instead of simply saying no, acknowledge its importance to them, and let them know that they will be able to have it when they're older. That gives them a dual message: there's light at the end of the tunnel, and they're not bad for wanting the privilege that they're not yet ready to have.

Learning to Wait

Adults live in a world of delayed gratification. Our paychecks come days or even weeks after we've done the work. We put in many hours practicing musical instruments or driving golf balls to improve our performance. We wait until the end of a meal to savor

---

[5] A few years ago, when I was on a national television talk show that dealt with discipline issues, a parent actually said that other adults shouldn't stop her two-year-old girl from wandering into the street to play. Apparently she thought that being hit by a car was a good way for a toddler to learn the consequences of her actions. Unfortunately, what we had here wasn't a discipline issue but a clear case of child abuse and neglect.

dessert, or shun it so that we can lose five pounds by the end of the month.

Investments of time and effort come much harder to young children, many of whom appear to live by the motto "I want it, and I want it now!" Given the choice between eating one jelly bean now and getting two jelly beans ten minutes from now, many young children find they just can't wait.

The ability to wait for rewards becomes increasingly important as children grow older. School is filled with delays of gratification. To be successful and graduate, many children must learn to forgo time on the baseball field in favor of studying multiplication tables. To get along with friends, they must learn to wait their turn at games and to share their toys.

Psychologists have found that some young children—especially boys—who have a lot of trouble waiting are likely to have difficulties in other areas later on. Boys who are impatient tend to be disruptive at home, disliked by their peers, and poor at solving interpersonal problems. It's unclear why girls who are impatient tend not to have the same pattern of problems.

There have been some very interesting laboratory experiments, many conducted by Dr. Walter Mischel at Columbia University, to measure the delay of gratification among young children. A typical experiment involves bringing a child into a room that contains, among other things, a bell. After the child and the experimenter spend some time together, the child is shown a pair of treats or small toys, one of which the child perceives as much better than the other.

The experimenter then explains that she has to leave the room for a few minutes, but that the child can call her back immediately by ringing the bell. The child is told that if he waits for the experimenter to return on her own, he'll get the better treat; if he rings the bell, he'll get the treat he doesn't like as much.

This experiment and others have found that those young children who are able to delay gratification the longest tended to approach the situation differently from those who rang the bell early and settled for the lesser reward. The children who waited usually distracted themselves by thinking about things other than the treats. Typically, they found something to play with while they were alone in the room.

Those who rang the bell early tended to focus their thoughts during the waiting period on the reward. In other words, it's easier for a child to wait for a cookie if he plays with a toy than if he simply stares at the cookie jar and thinks about how good the treat will taste.

Those children who came up with strategies to delay gratification in some of Dr. Mischel's studies had some surprising and long-term advantages over those who rang the bell soon after they were left alone. Ten years or more after they were tested, the children who could distract themselves were found to have done better academically and appeared to handle frustration better than their peers.

Although early patience and higher school performance were correlated, it's unclear whether the former causes the latter.[6] Still, it makes intuitive sense that teaching a child better skills at delaying gratification will help her later on.

TECHNIQUES FOR TEACHING PATIENCE

If you're trying to help your child become more patient and less frustrated, the first place to look is in the mirror. Young children are very sensitive to how their parents delay gratification. If you aren't patient in dealing with your own frustrations, your child will probably act that way, too.

Here are some things to try:

- Adjust your expectations to the age of your child and the situation. Remember that kindergartners have a very dif-

---

[6] This confusion of correlation with causation is one of the great traps that professionals and laypeople (including politicians and school administrators) routinely fall into. Think of it this way: tall people tend to play more basketball than short people. (A correlation.) That doesn't mean that playing a lot of basketball will make you taller. (A causation.)

ferent sense of time from teenagers. To a five-year-old, a
delay of an hour may seem like an eternity.

Remember that children become more patient as they
grow older. Also, most children become more impatient
when they're under stress.

- Suggest things for your child to think about while she's
waiting. Without such suggestions, many young children
focus their thoughts on things that will probably make
them more impatient, such as how good a piece of candy
will taste or how much fun it will be to play with a toy.
Teaching your child to distract herself when she has to
wait will make the waiting less frustrating.

- Get involved in projects with your child that require you
both to be patient. At first, these should be projects in
which the delays are measured in minutes, not hours or
days. As she becomes more proficient at postponing gratification, you can shift to longer, more complex projects.

Baking cookies together, for example, is a wonderful
way for your child to begin practicing patience. It may
feel like it takes a long time to go from mixing the dough
to letting the cookies cool once they're out of the oven,
but the child can see the steps involved in each stage,
and learn to distract herself for relatively short periods
of time. Most important, she gets to eat the results at
the end.

SPOILING CHILDREN

I've found that parental concerns about spoiling children tend to
be seasonal, with the greatest worries occurring during the latter
part of each year. Although I have no hard evidence to back this
up, I believe that a key factor is the change in acceptable and even

expected behavior. The last ten weeks of the year bring out the
avarice in most children. On Halloween they roam in gangs, extorting candy from neighbors.[7] Throughout November and Decem-
ber they are bombarded by television commercials telling them
which toys and games will be necessary for social survival when
Christmas or Hanukkah comes. The watchwords of the season are
"Gimme, gimme, gimme!"

A friend of mine, who's a family therapist, told me how his
seven-year-old daughter had been so overwhelmed by the holiday
gifts she received that she stopped playing with the majority of
them within a week. Both he and his wife were concerned about
whether they were spoiling their daughter—although they used
very different standards (based on their own upbringings) for making that judgment. On the one hand, they didn't want her to feel
deprived relative to her peers. On the other, they didn't want to
become a rubber stamp of approval for everything their daughter
wanted.

Being spoiled is more than just a matter of being immature and
self-centered. All children have those traits to varying degrees. Nor
is it a matter of overindulgence. Indulged children know the
boundaries of acceptable behavior; spoiled children do not.

Parents are sometimes inappropriately concerned about
whether their children are spoiled. This is especially true for the
parents of young children who want to touch everything around
them, and who often refuse to share their new toys with friends or
siblings. They act as if possession is ten tenths of the law. When
they enter a store—especially a toy store—they immediately want
everything in sight.

But this is not selfishness or a sign of being spoiled. It's a natural and adaptive response. Even for children in kindergarten or
the first grade, wanting to touch, own, and play with everything
they see helps them learn the fundamentals of how the world
works.

Older children have already mastered much of the information

---

[7] It's amazing how few children (and adults) realize that by saying "Trick or
treat?" children are actually offering you an option.

to be gained by simply touching and playing with objects. They are always in search of new experiences, repeatedly asking adults to buy them things. They must have a particular game or doll, they say. But when asked why this need is so pressing, they rarely have a good reason.

This is a more sophisticated behavior than it appears, for it allows children to test their power relative to their parents and other adults, and to determine the acceptable limits of their behavior. It is also a chance for them to practice their skills at negotiating in a safe environment. A friend may reject and leave you if you are too demanding; a parent will not.

My friend the family therapist recognized this in his daughter. He reported feeling a lot of pressure from her to buy things whenever they went into a store with her. But the underlying issue seemed to be her ability to coerce him into buying something rather than her wanting that particular item.

Parents who fail to recognize that distinction are most likely to have spoiled children who constantly demand gifts from them. Giving in, even when done with the best of intentions, creates a paradox for both parent and child. When parents grant children's unreasonable requests, it doesn't do what the parents hope it will do: quench the child's desires. Instead, it brings about *more* unreasonable requests from the child. It also creates anxiety for the children, since they still don't know what their limits are.

Being spoiled can have a profound effect on how children relate to their peers as well as to their parents. Spoiled children tend not to share things well. Nobody wants to play with them. It can lead to long-term problems as adolescents and even adults.

This doesn't mean you should never give in to your child's heart-felt plea for the latest doll outfit or video game. Indulging children is one of the true joys of being a parent. Remember that you can give children lots of things as long as you give them time, love, and limits.

UNSPOILING A CHILD

One of the most powerful indicators that children are too selfish or self-centered often comes from their classmates at school. While parents may overlook the problem, a child's peers do not. If your child has no friends—and especially if you find yourself buying things for your child that you or he believe will dramatically increase his popularity—you should look into whether spoiling is the underlying issue.

There are several things you can do if you want to prevent your child from becoming spoiled, or want to help a spoiled child develop new and more appropriate habits:

- Try not to use material rewards, such as toys, to control behavior. Children learn to use those same techniques to gain control over their parents. They'll say things like "Look, I've been good. Give me the fancy toy truck."

- Find positive nonmaterial ways to reward your children. Recognize that your children will want and enjoy a gift of your time and attention more than the gift of an object. Be sure that when you do pay attention to your child, you're able to focus all of your concentration on him.

- Remember that children, like adults, value the things they have earned more than the things they are given. Most children are thrilled to work with their parents to solve the problem of how to get something that they would really like.

OTHER PARENTS' STANDARDS

Not liking or trusting the parents of your children's friends can be an awkward situation. The problem may be as dramatic as a concern for your child's safety around parents who abuse alcohol or other drugs, or who simply do not watch the children closely. It may center on your child's emotional welfare, such as when the friend's parents are constantly arguing or are verbally abusive. Or it may be as mundane as a disagreement over whether the children should be allowed to have candy and potato chips before dinner.

A friend of mine once told me how she would cringe whenever she thought of her ten-year-old daughter visiting a particular classmate's home. The problem lay not with the other child but with the child's parents, who had a strikingly different approach to supervising children. The classmate's parents didn't seem to have any rules or provide any guidance at all to children who visited. My friend believed that her daughter needed structure. She said that neither her daughter nor her classmate was organized or mature enough to handle that much freedom.

She knew that refusing to let her daughter play with that classmate was likely to backfire. The other girl would appear all the more attractive because she was forbidden fruit. She solved the problem by allowing the two girls to play together at her home or at school, but not allowing her daughter to go to the classmate's house.

While my friend's concerns were based on child development and safety issues, sometimes parents' worries stem from differences in philosophy and values. For example, one family may be politically liberal while the other is archconservative. Parents may even admit that there is nothing wrong with the beliefs of a new friend's family; they simply disagree with those beliefs. Unlike concerns about safety and emotional welfare, the occurrence of this type of problem is often a reflection of your child's stage of development.

Befriending someone outside their normal social circle is one way that children test how their parents respond to their growing ability to think independently. Will they be allowed to make more of their own decisions and reach their own conclusions about important issues in their lives? Recognizing those tests for what they are will allow parents to avoid unnecessary battles while encouraging their children's independence.

A psychologist described to me two parents who contacted her because they were concerned about their eleven-year-old daughter's growing friendship with a family across the street. The parents of the eleven-year-old were agnostic, and became upset when their daughter started bringing home religious tracts and asking to go with her friend to a vacation Bible school. They worried that the friend's family was having an undue influence on their child.

The psychologist counseled the parents to avoid taking sides and to allow their daughter to make up her own mind. Forbidding the child to see the friend or to talk about religion would likely encourage the girl to side even more closely with the other family. One reason is that children this age not only identify strongly with their peers, but routinely test their own independence by challenging their parents. It is part of their necessary preparation for separation.

The parents permitted their child to emulate her girlfriend's behavior of reading the Bible and religious tracts every night. They also discussed the topic with her. Once she could do that, she lost interest, because there was nothing to fight with her parents about. Allowing the girl to make up her mind (especially since the situation involved philosophy rather than safety) also answered her underlying question about whether her parents recognized her growing maturity.

HANDLING DIFFERENT STANDARDS

There are several things that you should keep in mind when you have concerns about the parents of your children's friends:

- Do not compromise on issues of physical safety or emotional welfare. Problems that involve your child's safety or emotional health require a definite and unified stand from both parents. For example, parents should not feel pressured to allow their children to visit friends whose parents provide inadequate supervision. School-age children are often made uncomfortable by the problems at a friend's home, but do not know how to handle the situations.

In fact, children this age sometimes say they're glad their parents won't let them visit a particular child's house. It relieves them of the decisions and allows them to blame their parents for it. That way, the parents can look like the bad guys so that the children don't have to, and therefore don't risk losing the friendship.

• Remember that children are often tremendously loyal to their friends. This may be due in part to the shift in the types of friendships that occurs in late elementary school. Until that age, a child's friends are perhaps better described as playmates. They are chosen largely out of convenience: they live nearby or attend the same school. Around age ten, children begin to choose friends the way adults do: because of shared values and perceptions of the world.

If your disagreement with the other parents is philosophical, it is often better to remain silent. If you openly criticize the friend or the friend's parents, that may backfire. Your child will often want to stick up for his friends and their parents, no matter what the issue.

• Decide how you will communicate your concerns to the other parents if it becomes necessary. You can deal with less serious concerns directly or indirectly. Concerns about supervision, for example, can be discussed parent-to-parent. But problems like physical abuse or drug use require professional help. If you feel that your child's friend is in a dangerous or abusive situation, talk to the principal of the child's school.

Some problems that concern you may also concern other parents. Raising the issue at a PTA meeting or other community group can often lead to a consensus among parents in a school or neighborhood about rules that everyone agrees to follow, like no unsupervised parties and no alcohol for adolescents. This approach also allows parents to see how their standard operating procedures compare with those of others in their community.

• Don't worry about small differences between families in rules or child-rearing practices. A few ounces of junk food or an extra hour of television or video games is unlikely to have any lasting effect, although your children may request those things at home. (For countless generations, parents have listened to their children's heartfelt cries of "But Bobby's mom lets him do it!" even when Bobby's mother has never done anything of the sort.)

Children can distinguish between and adapt to different rules in different settings. After all, the rules for behaving in school are quite different from the rules for behaving at home. Learning that different homes have different standards and expectations is the same.

• Don't overestimate the influence of the parents of your child's friend. It's easy to make such a mistake, especially since some parents tend to believe they are a strong and positive influence over their own children's friends. But the effect of the other child's parents on your child is probably very small. It's the other child who's important to your child, not the parents.

7

Behavior Problems

A little inaccuracy sometimes saves tons of explanation.
—SAKI (H. H. MUNRO) (1870–1916)

I remember a letter—clearly apocryphal—that was posted on a bulletin board at my dormitory when I was in college. It was supposedly written by a freshman to her parents just before the Christmas break. In it, she described in vivid detail how, instead of attending college as her parents had been supposing, she had spent the past three months living with her new boyfriend, an unemployed high school dropout who occasionally hit her when he was drunk. He had gotten her pregnant and had just been arrested for selling drugs. It was a pathetic and, to any parent, terrifying set of images.

The concluding paragraph of the letter, however, went something like this: "Actually, Mom and Dad, none of what I've written in this letter is true. I have been attending college since September. It's just that I got a 'D' in my history course, and I wanted to put it in perspective for you. Love, your daughter."

We all sometimes need that new perspective when interpreting and responding to our children's behaviors—especially those behaviors we don't appreciate. Understanding the reasons why school-age children occasionally lie, cheat, steal, and otherwise get into trouble will help you react appropriately and constructively when your own child inevitably experiments with those behaviors. I've explored academic cheating and possible responses to it in Chapter 2. In this chapter we'll take a look at some other common behavior problems of children this age, as well as how children interpret and react to the lies adults tell them.

Lying by Children

Lying is a skill all children learn. It is a tool for avoiding blame or punishment, and for shoring up a poor self-image. While all children lie, some do it much more than others. Psychologists who study lying have found patterns that help predict which children will lie the most.

The key difference appears to be the emotional well-being of the child. Children who are chronic liars don't feel good about themselves. Even so, repeated lying can be a sign of several underlying problems, each of which requires a different response from parents.

The most common reason for lying, particularly among younger children, is a fear of punishment. This is especially true when the punishment is severe or the parents have unrealistically high expectations for their children. For example, a colleague told me about a family she had been counseling. The five-year-old girl's stepfather insisted that she do such things as putting away all her clothes without being asked, and clearing the table after dinner. He punished her if she didn't. The girl would say she had done the chores, even if she'd (predictably) forgotten.

Although the stepfather complained about the girl's lying, the underlying issue was his inappropriate expectations of what a normal five-year-old could do. The child was handling the situation the best way she knew how. Given her limited abilities and powerlessness within the family, lying was actually an adaptive response.

Older school-age children will also lie to enhance their self-esteem and social status. For example, they may claim to have met a particular rock star, actor, or sports figure, or they may exaggerate their parents' wealth. Occasional lies like this are seldom anything to worry about, since they're to be expected in the course of children's games of one-upmanship.

But repeated lies about social status are a sign of trouble. They tell you that the child has a bad attitude about himself. Ask yourself why he might be feeling humiliated or worthless. Is he being ignored? Has he been the butt of jokes, or been belittled?

For older children, chronic lying is often a rebellion against restrictions. It is a way to challenge a parent's authority. Preteens no longer feel they must tell their parents everything they do; they may respond with a lie to what they perceive as an intrusive question.

As they grow older, children realize that the greatest control they can have is the control of information. Generally, the more intrusive or overinvolved parents are, the more likely it is that pre-adolescents will lie by omitting information. Often they do this blatantly, as if to emphasize their growing need for privacy. *"Where did you go?"* "Nowhere." *"What did you do?"* "Nothing." *"Who was there?"* "Nobody you'd know."

A sudden increase in lying can also be a signal that something's wrong in the family. This is especially true if the child is acting out in other ways, such as stealing or committing vandalism. You should pay particular attention if the victims of the thefts or other petty crimes are other family members. Often this is a cry for help that is much louder than his words alone could be.

For example, it's not too unusual when counseling a preadolescent who has done something dramatic and new, such as stealing and crashing the family car, or who has been arrested for burglary, to discover that his parents were contemplating a divorce. Creating this crisis was the only way the child could think of to reunite his parents, if only for the moment. While his motivations were unconscious, his actions addressed his strong needs.

RESPONDING TO LIES

I've always found it useful to remember that, from a child's perspective, a lie is simply the best solution to a problem that he can come up with at that moment. The real challenge for the parents of chronic liars isn't spotting the lies, but finding the underlying issues and helping the child learn different and more appropriate responses. Here are some ideas that may help:

- Ask yourself if you're giving your child permission to tell the truth. Remember that children most often lie to avoid punishment. What does your child think you'll do if he tells you what really happened?

  Even though, as adults, we can't be forced to testify against ourselves in a court of law, we routinely ask our children to do just that. Children often tell psychologists and teachers that they felt guilty and wanted to tell their parents what they had done, but they saw that their parents were in a bad mood when they came home, and worried about the punishment they might receive if they didn't lie.

  One way to encourage your children to tell you the truth is to focus your responses on their specific behaviors (breaking the heirloom vase) rather than on their characters ("You never listen to me when I tell you not to play ball in the house!"). Give them a chance to make appropriate amends when they've done something wrong so that they don't feel that they'll be punished forever if they tell you the truth.

- Look for patterns in lying as clues to what's really going on. These patterns can be in the situations where children lie, as well as the content of those lies. For example, you should be more concerned if your child routinely lies in several settings, such as in school or with friends, as well as at home. A child who has problems with self-esteem is more likely to lie in a variety of situations, but a child who's afraid of punishment will lie mostly to the people he's afraid of.

- Remember that lying is an act that involves at least two people, not just your child. If you want your child to stop lying to you, you'll have to change as well. Ask yourself if your own patterns of lying have given your child the message that it's all right for him to lie.

  Have the restrictions you've placed on your children's activities changed as they've gotten older? For example, a child in late elementary school will want more control over how he spends his weekly allowance than younger children do. Let's say you've told him that you don't want him to "waste his money" on comic books. If you later ask him how he got the *Spider Man* comic that's in his room, he'll probably lie.

  The most realistic solution to the problem is to let him buy the comics. (See Chapter 2 for other reasons why you should actually encourage him to buy them.) This is an important way of recognizing that he's growing up. Besides, buying comics is pretty innocuous and is probably even beneficial; it's a much better choice than spending his allowance on cigarettes, alcohol, or illegal drugs—substances that are increasingly used by school-age children. (Kids are less likely to ask to do really outrageous things if you've allowed them to do at least a few semi-outrageous things.)

- Don't tempt your child to lie. If you know your child forgot to feed the dog, don't ask him if he did so. If your child begins by lying to you, don't let him continue and dig himself in deeper. Instead, stop him and let him know that you know he's lying.

  Remember that it's better to assume the role of an educator than the role of a police officer. Help your child learn how to accomplish what he wants without lying to do so. Show him how he might tell you the truth. (While this may be obvious to you, it may not be to him.) Explain that telling you what really happened offers him a chance to correct the situation at least partway. If all children learn is that they'll be punished when you catch them lying, they'll simply become better liars.

LYING TO CHILDREN

Before we're too quick to criticize our children for lying, it's important to remember that the truths we tell our children are punctuated with lies. We insist that all their drawings are beautiful or that we're not really upset by the problems at our work. We tell them lies to protect them or to protect ourselves. And we deceive them about Santa Claus and the Tooth Fairy so that we can enjoy their childhood a little more.

Most of the deceptions are benign and have few if any long-lasting consequences. Yet children learn a great deal from the lies they are told by their parents and others who are important to them. What they learn often depends upon how they interpret the act of lying, rather than the lie itself.

For example, a psychologist I know counseled a man who had been in trouble with the Internal Revenue Service. The man had always wanted to appear as a hero to his children. Rather than admit that he was having difficulties, he tried to hide his plight from them. Eventually, his children discovered the lie and became very cynical about their father's behavior. They were much more upset that he had lied to them than by anything else he had done to cause the problems. His attempts at being a hero had backfired.

Young children often interpret a parent's lie as the parent's not caring about them because there's something fundamentally wrong with them as children. That's why even some trivial lies by parents can be so upsetting to children. They can also have the same reaction to lies by other important adults in their lives.[1] For example, if a child knows he is not doing well in school, but is repeatedly told by the teacher that he is doing fine, he's more likely to stop believing the teacher in other areas than to think his own school performance is good. To the child, the adult's lie is an important and painful reflection of their relationship.

Children as young as five years will tell you that parents in general lie, but they deny that their own parents lie. (Research by Dr. William Damon at Brown University has shown that children don't start talking about their own parents' lies until they reach adolescence.) This behavior is similar to how children will say that parents have sex, but their own parents don't.

Dr. Michael Lewis, the director of the Institute for the Study of Child Development at the Robert Wood Johnson Medical School in New Jersey, has found that adult lies tend to fall into one of three categories: self-deception, self-protection, and so-called white lies which are told to spare the feelings of the listener. His studies have shown that when women lie, they're more likely to do so to spare the feelings of another person. When men lie, they are more likely to be protecting themselves or to be deceiving themselves.

Children's interpretations of the motives behind such adult lies can also lead them to forgive their parents. For example, in one study of approximately five hundred elementary school students in New York and Iowa, the researchers found that, on average, children stopped believing in Santa Claus around age seven and a half. But many children kept up the charade after they knew the truth because, they said, they did not want to disappoint their parents.

None of the children who were interviewed said they were unhappy or upset by their parents' having lied about Santa Claus. The most common response to finding out the truth was that they felt older and more mature. They felt proud that they now knew something that the younger kids didn't.

---

[1] This same type of thinking can be seen in children whose parents are considering divorce. Children naturally blame themselves for many things that are simply out of their control. It's another example of their inherent egocentrism.

BEING CAUGHT IN A LIE

Having your child catch you in a lie can be upsetting for both of you. Children take their parents' and teachers' lies seriously. Here are several things you can do to help your children come to terms with adults' lies:

- Look at the emotional message that went along with the lie. Remember that children see lies as reflections of your underlying relationship. Children become particularly upset when they feel that their emotions are being trivialized or discounted, such as when you tell your child that he shouldn't be nervous about attending a new school or going off to summer camp for the first time.

- Ask yourself about the symbolic meaning of the lie. Children are much more forgiving of large but benevolent lies like Santa Claus and the Easter Bunny than they are of trivial lies about the store being out of the ice cream you had promised them when, in reality, you'd simply forgotten to look. By lying about a relatively small issue, you're discounting the value of both their desires and your promise.

- Be honest about having lied. This is especially important if you were lying to protect your child or someone else. Remember, however, that children generally do not understand the social reasons for white lies until they are about six years old.

  Don't simply ignore your child's having caught you in a lie. If you do so, your child's suspicions and concerns about your integrity in other areas will grow. Instead, you should apologize and explain, just as you'd expect your child to do.

  The one exception to this, however, is a benevolent lie about a cultural myth. Young children may have an emotional need to maintain these myths after they have intellectually realized that the myths are not true. Rather than simply blurting out the truth when your child asks whether Santa Claus is real, turn the question around. Ask her whether *she* thinks Santa Claus is real. The answer she gives will tell you what she needs to hear from you at that moment.

STEALING

A few crayons from a kindergarten classroom find their way into your daughter's lunch box. A friend's toy mysteriously migrates to your son's collection. Your ten-year-old furtively hides a candy bar in his coat pocket as he walks out of the store.

Shoplifting and petty thievery are perhaps the most common crimes perpetrated by children. The issue is not the value of what is taken, for that is often minimal, but the thoughts behind the behavior. Children's perceptions of stealing are determined by their stage of development as well as by their parents' reactions to the stealing.

For toddlers and preschoolers, there's no malice at work when they pocket their playmates' toys. Children that age simply haven't mastered the difference between wishing something were theirs and being entitled to have it. From their perspective, wanting an item badly enough gives them a claim to it.

Before entering kindergarten, however, children usually develop the notion of private ownership and the recognition that specific amounts of money must be used to buy something from a store. It's a difficult concept that takes several years to understand. By the time they're in school, however, they should have the inner controls that prevent them from simply taking an object they covet—at least most of the time.

Although it's important to treat petty theft by children as serious business, you should remember that it's not necessarily a step toward a life of crime. While nearly all adult criminals committed petty theft when they were young, so did most people who grew up to be law-abiding.

There's also a big difference between one or two instances of petty theft and repeated instances of thievery in childhood. Research by Dr. Lewis P. Lipsitt at Brown University has found that young children at risk for later and more serious problems with the law tend to respond differently when they're caught red-handed. Those children at greatest risk seem to be the ones who persistently deny their involvement despite all the evidence.[2] The intensity of their denial is the tip-off that there may be a problem.

While young children will justify their behavior simply by saying they wanted what they stole, older children will excuse their thievery in other ways: the store wanted too much money for the item; the company expects a certain amount of theft; the clerk was rude. This need to rationalize their behavior is, ironically, a reflection of their increased moral development and awareness of societal rules.

Among school-age children, petty theft is sometimes a sign of a more serious problem, although not a lack of moral development. Repeated shoplifting may be a cry for help, especially if the children aren't secretive about what they've stolen. Brazenly wearing a stolen sweater may be the only way a child feels comfortable calling attention to other difficulties at home or at school. The child knows that by behaving this way he can be referred for psychological help in handling other issues like a death in the family or a parent's divorce, without appearing weak (or feeling he has betrayed a family secret) by admitting his need for this support.

---

[2] Remember, however, that such blatant denial is both normal and typical for a younger child such as a three-year-old, who's still engaging in what psychologists call magical thinking. They have trouble differentiating between doing something bad and being someone bad. They act as if denying their involvement is the only way they can avoid seeing themselves, and having their parents view them, as someone bad. By the time children are in grade school, they should no longer be thinking or acting this way.

RESPONDING TO STEALING

The first rule in dealing with a child who has stolen something is to make it clear that you don't approve. If you rationalize your child's stealing by calling it borrowing or a misunderstanding, your child won't understand what he's done wrong.

You should make an immediate, forceful, and appropriate response, not because you're afraid that your child will fall into a life of crime, but because this is the time to talk about values in a way that's directly linked to your child's behavior. That's much more powerful than giving your child an abstract lecture about what to do and what not to do in life.

Here are some steps you might consider taking:

- Adjust your response to the age of your child. With a kindergartner, you might say something like, "I see that you have Tommy's truck here. That belongs to him. He must be missing it. We should take it back to Tommy's house."

   That points up the problem, helps the child identify with the other person's emotions, and states the solution. With older children, you can talk about the larger issues of theft and trustworthiness. ("If people think you might be stealing from them, they won't want to be your friends. Would you want a friend who took your stuff?")

- Have your child make restitution. This means not only immediately returning, replacing, or paying for the stolen objects, but suffering some other consequence as well, such as having to do extra chores. Also, if your child has stolen something from a store, help him see the store as more than a faceless institution. Many children don't understand how thefts affect the people who own and work in stores.

- Put your child on notice. Let him know you'll be watching him closely. Keep your child out of situations that may be too tempting. Don't leave him unsupervised in stores. Ask to see receipts. Make sure your child knows that you're monitoring his possessions. That doesn't mean you'll be a snoop, but that you'll pay extra attention to new or unusual items.

  If the theft was significant or part of a pattern, tell your child that as his parent you have the right to search his room and possessions (in his presence) if you have reason to believe he's still stealing. This underscores how seriously you regard theft.

OTHER PETTY CRIMES

For many children and preadolescents, experimenting with petty crime is a part of growing up. It may be a way to fit in with a group or to test the limits of acceptable behavior. To the child, taking a "five-finger discount" on some makeup at the drugstore or spray-painting a name on a wall may seem relatively harmless, especially when compared with violent crimes.

But psychologists and criminologists urge parents to pay close attention to such incidents, for they may be the child's cry for help with other issues. There are patterns of behavior that predict which children treat delinquency as a passing phase, and which graduate to more serious crimes as adolescents and adults.

As I said earlier, you generally shouldn't be overly concerned by a single instance of shoplifting, curfew violation, or the like.

Surveys of adolescents show that up to 70 percent admit to having done things like this. (A significant proportion of the other 30 percent may be lying.)

Not being concerned doesn't mean ignoring the problem, of course. But your response should be in line with the extent of the problem. Overreacting with severe and inappropriate punishments may make matters worse for children who are simply testing limits. Underreacting to children who are at high risk may mean they don't get the help they need to break the cycle.

One of the best and most obvious predictors of later criminal behavior is the frequency with which a child gets into trouble with the law. (Twice within a year is a sign of a potentially big problem.) The type of delinquent behavior is also important. There's a big difference between the children who commit property crimes and those who commit crimes against people.

The younger a child is when he engages in violent or delinquent behavior, the more likely it is that the child will get into more serious trouble later. According to Dr. Denise Gottfredson of the Institute of Criminal Justice and Criminology at the University of Maryland, certain personality characteristics are also associated with children who engage in repeated antisocial behavior. She's found that impulsivity, sensation-seeking, and defiance are all stable traits found among juvenile delinquents that can sometimes be seen as early as preschool.

That doesn't mean that a young child who has these traits is destined for a life of crime. Rather, children who act that way are at higher risk for criminal behavior later if they are exposed to certain environmental conditions, such as the likelihood of being unemployed after leaving school or a high amount of violence in their families.

Children who commit petty crimes as part of a group also warrant closer attention than those who act alone. Preadolescents crave acceptance by their peers. This desire to fit in makes them vulnerable to accepting antisocial values and behavior if, in exchange, they gain attention and recognition. That's one of the attractions of youth gangs: they help children feel important when they believe the larger world is ignoring them.

RESPONDING TO DELINQUENCY

Here are some things you can do if your child gets in trouble with the law, especially if it happens more than once:

- Don't write it off as simply sowing some wild oats. Go for outside help. Get some advice from a school guidance counselor. Intervene early. The longer you wait, the more difficult it will be to correct the problem.

- Give your child a chance to make things right. If he's shoplifted some sporting goods, he should not only return them, but should, in addition, do some free work for the owner or manager of the store. That lets your child clean the slate.

- Don't go overboard with punishment. An overly harsh response to a minor infraction may do little more than make your child more rebellious. For example, grounding your child for a month is impractical, if not impossible. It also allows him to stay upset with you instead of focusing on what he did wrong.

  Remember that children thrive on responsibility. They want to feel that you recognize their growing maturity. At the same time, they may need to be shown more acceptable ways of expressing their anger or of fitting in with a different crowd.

  Instead of trying to stop your child from doing these things, which you really can't control, tell him that you're trying to help him stop himself from behaving this way because you care about him and you know he is capable and behaving well.

- Check out your child's peer group. This is difficult with older children, since they have so much more control over where they go and whom they see. But if your child is getting into trouble, it's the first thing you should look into. One of the biggest correlates of delinquent behavior

is hanging around with other children who are delinquent. Monitor your child's friends. Don't be afraid to
question your child about whom he's spending time with.
Ask him to invite his friends to your home so that you
can meet them. You should be concerned if your child
has a friend whom he doesn't want you to meet.

PHYSICAL AGGRESSION

What should you do if your child comes home with scraped knuckles and a bloody nose, obviously results of a fistfight? Does it matter if your child threw the first punch? What if your child claims
to have been standing up for his (or your) good name, or defending
a friend who was being picked on? Should your response or expectations be different if your child is a girl?

While the occasional schoolyard scuffle is seldom anything to
worry about, there are some young children who repeatedly express themselves with their fists. Child psychiatrists and psychologists are paying closer attention to these school-age frequent
fighters, for they have found that such aggressive behavior often
leads to later trouble and may be a sign of seemingly unrelated
problems. Studies have shown that children who get into a lot of
fights in elementary school are more likely to get involved earlier
in sex and to experiment with drugs and alcohol.

This is especially true for boys, since they are much more likely
to scrap it out with a classmate than girls are. Even at a young
age, girls tend to settle their disagreements with words instead of
brute force. In fact, repeated fighting in a ten-year-old girl, for
example, is often a tip-off to underlying biological and emotional
problems such as depression.

According to research by Dr. Kenneth A. Dodge of Vanderbilt
University, almost all adolescents and young adults who are in
repeated trouble with the law had behavior problems in early elementary school. Again, the converse—that children who have

early behavior problems will later get into repeated trouble with the law—is not necessarily true. Dr. Dodge has found that only about half of the children who get into a lot of trouble in elementary school are likely to show antisocial behavior as adults. Still, such early problems warrant greater attention by parents and teachers.

How parents and teachers should intervene depends largely on the reasons for the repeated fighting. Focusing solely on the punching and shoving without addressing the underlying causes sometimes only makes matters worse.

For some children, chronic aggressive behavior may be a sign of a learning disability. Their aggression seems to reflect their frustration in the classroom and, perhaps, their rejection by teachers and classmates. Beating someone up may be the best way they can think of at that moment to raise their self-esteem and vent their frustrations.

Among other children, the fighting may be a sign of an emotional problem such as depression.[3] It may also be the child's response to difficulties within his family, such as an impending divorce or a severe financial crisis. Remember that children often blame themselves for problems at home that are, in reality, out of their control. They may feel, unconsciously, that they deserve to be punished for this. So they set themselves up to be beaten up by the school bullies, or they get into fights as a cry for help.

Perhaps the most common reason for excessive fighting, however, stems from how children, especially young boys, feel they are expected to behave when they are challenged or angry. In our culture, we give children mixed messages about fighting. We both abhor and revere physical aggression.

Television and video games are filled with images of people settling their disputes with violence. Many of the movies most popular with older school-age children send the message that we don't believe that we can resolve matters peacefully. In fact, some of

---

[3] There's a common misconception among parents and teachers that clinically depressed children walk around looking sad and withdrawn. In fact, depressed children and adolescents often appear irritable or angry.

them imply that physical aggression is a preferred first response or even the only honorable solution to a difficult conflict.

Children may also get the same idea from sources closer to home. Parents sometimes give the message that you have to knock down a certain number of people to be respected. In those situations, the real problems lie not with the children, but with the parents. The methods parents use to work out problems with each other are the methods that children are most likely to use when dealing with their peers.

That isn't to say that children who get into fistfights have parents who regularly duke it out at home. Rather, children learn general approaches to resolving conflict by watching their parents and other adults in their lives. How do you negotiate? When do you give in? How do you discern the other person's point of view? Can you admit when you're wrong?

When interviewed, many of the children who are in trouble with the law or are involved with gangs state that they feel they have no options for resolving conflict but fighting. That lack of perceived choices is a sign of trouble.

It's also compounded by the tremendous peer pressure to fight that's felt by older boys. To back down or to suggest a nonviolent resolution, especially if it is done in public, can be interpreted as a sign of weakness. To some children, losing face in front of friends can be more painful than the bruises from a fistfight.

It is, perhaps, unreasonable to expect children—especially boys in our culture—never to get into a fight with their peers. But there are patterns of frequency and timing that indicate that such fighting is a more serious problem for some children than for others.

Hitting someone is a primitive response to anger and frustration, so it's much more common among younger children who don't yet have the verbal and social skills to handle those situations in more sophisticated ways. That's why a single fight is less of a concern for kindergartners than for preadolescents. Also, you should be more concerned about a child whose aggression is impulsive, and when aggression is the way a child routinely responds to anger and frustration.

SETTLING CONFLICTS
WITHOUT VIOLENCE

A rule of thumb for deciding whether a child needs help because of his or her fighting is that the *earlier* the fighting occurs, and the *more locations* it takes place, and the *more frequent* the fights, the more parents should be concerned. Here are some things you can do to help a child who seems to be fighting all the time:

• Help your child analyze what happened. Get your child's account of what took place, especially the circumstances that led to the fight. Don't focus on who hit whom first. If your child didn't feel justified, he probably wouldn't have been in the fight in the first place.

Ask your child how he knew the situation was escalating. Talk about what he might have done at different points to prevent the fight. Remember that a child may need your permission *not* to fight. He may assume it's what you wanted him to do.

• Help your child learn new ways to handle conflict. Remember that some children go through a stage of getting into fights because they can't see other ways of responding to a challenge. Some elementary schools and after-school programs like the Boy Scouts and YWCAs offer programs that teach children nonviolent ways of resolving disputes. You can also teach them such techniques at home.

Do some role playing and problem solving with your child. Replay the situation that led to a recent fight, with each of you taking different roles. Explore other ways he might have handled it, and what the outcome might have been. Talk about alternatives to fighting. Let your child practice those skills with you before he has to try them away from home.

- Talk about issues of revenge. You can be pretty sure that the loser of the fight is fantasizing about ways to get even, and the winner is worried about just that. Children who have lost a fight and who are frightened may start carrying a weapon for protection, sometimes with disastrous results.

  Remember that serious disputes seldom stop with one fight unless you do something to break the cycle. Talk to your child about ways to avoid future fights while still saving face. Find out how others may have egged him on when the dispute was just starting. Discuss how he might respond to that type of social pressure in the future. Could he make a joke to defuse the tension? Should he forcefully state that he's not interested in fighting?

- Be careful how you punish a child for fighting. If you feel your child should be punished, make it something constructive, such as helping more at home. The punishment for fighting should never be spanking or hitting. That gives your child the message that you really do believe in violence for settling disputes.

- If your child's getting into more than a few fights, look for professional help. Chronic fighting is almost always a symptom of other problems. These can range from family stress to depression to learning disabilities. While the schoolyard battles may gain a child temporary prestige among his peers, the long-term social and academic consequences are serious. Many child guidance centers have programs to help these combative children to learn new ways of handling conflict and to cope with their underlying problems as well.

- Change the group of children your child spends time with after school. Children who are aggressive often hang out with other aggressive children, which can make matters worse. Look for ways you can get your child involved with a group that has different standards and expectations of behavior.

For aggressive children who have trouble following rules, team sports often give them a more appropriate way of getting out their aggressions while learning to play by rules. For children who are aggressive because they're impulsive, individual sports seem to help because they're learning self-control and self-discipline.

- Look at your own behavior. Ask yourself what you do when you're angry at your child or your spouse. That's the behavior you've been teaching. You can't expect your child to do anything different.

BULLIES

Most classrooms include at least one highly aggressive child who tries to have his way by bullying. While adults realize that such children are seldom as threatening as they try to make themselves out to be, their peers see them quite differently. A ten-year-old who is extorting milk money or threatening to chase a child home after school can loom large in the fears of an eight-year-old. Handing over a quarter a day to avoid possibly being beaten up seems a small price to pay.

Teachers and psychologists have recently become more sensitive to the effects of bullying on both the victims and the bullies themselves. Some schools are developing programs to teach more appropriate and effective social skills to both bullies and the children they chronically pick on.

Researchers have noticed patterns in the backgrounds of bullies and their repeated victims. Highly aggressive children tend to view the world as a more dangerous and hostile place than other children do. They're also more easily provoked into a physical response to a perceived problem. For example, an aggressive child who gets bumped while waiting in line for a drink will tend to interpret it as a hostile act. Other children will give the person who bumped them the benefit of the doubt. Still others will compliantly move over to let the bumper jostle ahead of them in line.

Highly aggressive behavior seldom disappears by itself. As children grow older, it often leads to academic trouble, as well as social and even legal problems. Some bullying can be brought on by crises at home, like a parent's loss of a job, a severe illness, or a divorce. Children often feel powerless and frustrated in those situations, but they worry that expressing their feelings directly toward their parents will only make matters worse. Instead, they choose much safer targets—like their classmates or younger children—on whom to test the limits of their power and control.

Research by Dr. David Perry of Florida Atlantic University has found that boys tend to become more aggressive in the first year or two after their parents divorce. This response doesn't seem to be common among younger girls, but it is seen among adolescent girls.[4]

Other studies have shown that bullies' parents generally behave differently from the parents of nonaggressive children. When they touch their children, they tend to be brusque and controlling, rather than reassuring. They use discipline inconsistently, often letting an infraction go on one occasion but punishing the child severely for it the next time.

The parents of aggressive children are also more likely to be physically or verbally aggressive toward each other, and to use corporal punishment when they don't like their children's behavior. Both of those behaviors reinforce the child's perception that aggression and violence are acceptable and appropriate solutions to problems.

---

[4] In general, aggression in girls in our culture is different from aggression in boys. Girls tend to be aggressive by excluding others and by saying mean things. Boys are aggressive by hitting and getting into fights.

IF YOUR CHILD'S A VICTIM

Although all children have run-ins with bullies on occasion, some are singled out repeatedly. Many adults think that these chronic victims of bullies are passive, shy children. But researchers say that's not always the case. Highly aggressive children, including bullies themselves, are at least as likely as nonaggressive children to be picked on repeatedly.

One reason is that aggressive children tend to be rejected by their classmates. They have difficulty forming friendships and spend much time alone. The social relationships they do form tend to be with other aggressive children.

The other group of chronic victims fits the stereotype of the insecure, socially isolated child. They tend to have poor self-esteem and a less well developed sense of humor than other children their age.

Being a victim is also what psychologist call a stable trait. If you're picked on in the third grade, you're likely to be picked on in the sixth grade too.

If your child is being picked on by a bully, here are some things you can do:

- Don't assume it's a major problem. Sometimes, rushing in to help will make a victim feel even more inadequate. Take your cues from your child's reaction. For some children, being bullied can be a traumatic and shameful experience. For others, the effects may be minimal and transitory.

- If your child is a regular victim of bullies, help him make more friends. Children make friends by sharing social experiences. Help your child plan an outing to a skating rink or a video arcade with one or two classmates. Have other children over to your home to play. Encourage your child to join organizations such as the Boy Scouts, a

band, or a karate club. Children who have a network of
friends tend not to be bullied.

- Rehearse with your child how he might react when
  threatened by a bully. The first response, if possible,
  should be for the child to tell a teacher or a playground
  monitor. Safety at school (which is probably the most
  common location for bullying) is fundamentally the responsibility of adults. While some victims of bullies may
  worry about being called tattletales because they talked to
  an adult, this seldom happens in this situation. Usually
  the other children in the class are relieved that someone
  spoke up about a bully.

  If telling an adult doesn't work, or if no adult is available to help, your child should use a series of escalating
  responses, beginning with ignoring the bully or forcefully
  telling him to stop. Fighting back, or otherwise responding at the bully's level, should be a last resort.

8

Sibling Relationships

Big sisters are the crabgrass in the lawn of life.
—Charles Schulz (b. 1922)

In his autobiography, Mark Twain wrote about how he and his younger brother, Henry Clemens, had opposite personalities, even when they were young children. Henry was a goody-goody who felt honor bound to report his brother's misdeeds and questionable adventures to their mother. Twain later used their childhood conflicts as the basis for part of *The Adventures of Tom Sawyer*.

Sibling relationships develop much greater depth during the school-age years, for that is when children begin to understand the social and emotional implications of having brothers and sisters.

Before getting into the practical details of sibling relationships, such as how to handle rivalry, I'd like to spend a little time exploring how parents perceive siblings, and may grow to prefer one child to another—at least for a short period of time. Such preferences can be a cause of unnecessary guilt, especially for those parents who feel they must deal equally with all their children.

Few things demonstrate the natural diversity within families as clearly as the temperamental differences between siblings. The first child in a family may be highly gregarious; the second one, shy and demure. A bookworm may be sandwiched between two athletes, or vice versa.

While some of these differences take years to develop, others are apparent soon after birth. In fact, if you go into a newborn nursery, you'll hear parents talk about how their day-old child is different from his or her sibling.

According to Dr. Stephen Bank, a psychologist at Wesleyan University who studies sibling relationships, parents tend to see more extreme differences between their first- and second-born children than between other pairs of children in their families. That's an interesting phenomenon, since there's absolutely no biological reason why they should be any more or less different. It appears to reflect the parents' expectations more than the children's behaviors.

Differences in personalities shouldn't be surprising. Temperament appears to be largely genetic. While children share genes with their parents, the number of possible combinations of those genes leads to siblings who differ not only in physical characteristics like hair and eye color, but also in how generally grumpy or happy they are, and how easily they make the transition from one activity to another. In fact, two siblings are almost as likely to be different temperamentally as two children who are chosen at random.

HANDLING TEMPERAMENTAL DIFFERENCES

Research by Dr. Judy Dunn[1] at Pennsylvania State University has shown that siblings who are temperamentally different when they are young tend to have more quarrels than siblings who are similar. This can add to the stress of any household, especially if you're struggling against your chil-

---

[1] Dr. Dunn is also the mother of fraternal twin boys, whom she describes as "as different as chalk from cheese."

dren's temperaments instead of trying to work with them.

The first principle in handling children who are temperamentally different is to acknowledge and even celebrate the differences. Having one child who's shy and another who's bold doesn't mean you've done anything wrong in the way you've raised either one. These are largely inborn traits. Remember that you're relatively powerless to change your children's temperaments.[2] It's not your fault that you can't quickly turn a generally cranky child into a happy-go-lucky one.

Here are some other things to keep in mind when you're dealing with your children's relationships with their siblings:

- Don't force togetherness on your children. This will usually breed resentment instead of closeness. Let them enjoy their own activities and pursue their individual interests when possible. While this is a good idea for all siblings, it's especially important if they have widely disparate temperaments.

- Be flexible in your own interests and activities. Just as siblings have differing temperaments and interests, so do parents. Imposing your own fascination for cooking, baseball, or model trains on your offspring may work well with one child but be disastrous with another.

  Remember that it's almost always easier for adults than for children to participate in activities they find boring or don't enjoy. Such tolerance is a sign of maturity. Try to meet your children where their interests are instead of just trying to get them to change. Time spent sharing activities with a parent helps forge a strong relationship, which is more important than whether you're tossing a

---

[2] That doesn't mean that temperaments are immutable. While temperamental traits tend to show little change from one year to the next, there can be significant change over the course of a half-dozen years or more. Your fussy first grader isn't doomed to a life of crabbiness.

football, coloring pictures, or working on a computer together.

PLAYING FAVORITES

The statement that "I love each of my children equally" rings hollow to any parent who has more than one child. It is an impossible goal. More important, it is an inappropriate one as well.

We can, perhaps, see this best at its extreme. A few years ago I interviewed a psychiatrist for one of my *New York Times* "Parent & Child" columns. She told me of a woman she had been treating who had 11 children between the ages of 2 and 20. The mother was very concerned about treating (i.e., loving) each of her children equally. She showed it one Christmas by giving each of them a bicycle! It was a completely inappropriate choice which showed how her pathological concern about favoritism made her overlook the individual needs and wants of her children.

A psychologist I interviewed for another column told me of a family she was treating in which the son felt that his older sister was clearly his parents' favorite. The girl received lots of praise at home for getting good grades and having friends of whom the parents approved. The boy felt that no matter how well he did in school or how nicely he behaved, he couldn't compete.

In response, he decided on an unconscious level that his special talent and way to get attention was by failing. He was right, of course—at least about the second part. As soon as he started flunking courses and not showing up at school, his parents started paying much more attention to him than to his sister. It was not the type of attention he would have preferred, but it was better from his perspective than feeling ignored.

While the boy's reaction was extreme, his underlying feelings are common. There's an inherent rivalry between children for their parents' affection and attention. It's a high-stakes game, especially for younger children who glean much of their sense of self-worth from how their parents and other important adults, such as teachers, treat them.

That's not to say that all children's feelings of favoritism are necessarily destructive. In fact, a certain amount of unequal treatment of children may show that the parents recognize them as individuals, and are trying to meet their specific needs.

According to research by Dr. Stephen Bank of Wesleyan University, most people report that there was favoritism in their families as they were growing up. But children from the same family often don't agree on which child was favored.

One reason is that in many families, different children are placed in the limelight at different times. Newborns are often the center of their parents' attention. A year later, those same parents may seem to focus on an older child who's excelling at school or in sports, or one who's having problems. Similarly, parents may favor or subtly shun one of their sons or daughters because parent and child are temperamentally similar or different. An outgoing and gregarious parent, for instance, may feel less comfortable with a child who is generally shy and introspective than with one who is more boisterous.

While it's easy to focus on each child's temperament as a potential source of parental joy or frustration, what's more important is how parents perceive and interpret the temperamental differences in their children. It is seldom the temperament itself that sets off a parent's emotions, but the association of that temperament with themselves or with someone from their past.

For example, an aspect of a young girl's personality may remind her mother of a favorite aunt. Because of this, the mother may pay more attention to the girl or may seem to favor her over the other children in the family.

Parents don't always favor the child who's most like them. Sometimes we react negatively to a child who's like us in ways that make us uncomfortable. A son's shyness may be the cause of seemingly disproportionate anger from a mother because it is a trait that reminds her of herself as a young girl. The anger stems not only from the painful memories of her own shyness, but also from a desire for her son to somehow make up for her own childhood awkwardness and loneliness.[3]

The reasons for such emotions can sometimes reflect a child's stage of development. A sedate, low-key parent may enjoy being with a first grader who is learning to read, but have problems dealing with the predictable defiance of a preadolescent or the boundless energy of a toddler.

I remember a conversation with a child psychiatrist who told me how, at that moment, both he and his wife strongly preferred their seven-year-old daughter to her five-year-old sister. The younger girl was going through a stage of melodramatic pouting and being thin-skinned—traits both parents found annoying. They knew, based on their experience with the older child, that their feelings were temporary. They'd feel much less frustrated by their younger daughter as soon as she could learn, with their help, new and better ways of handling her frustrations.

My colleague's candor was refreshing. For many parents, the mere thought that they may like one child more than another is disquieting, as if it were a sure sign of their failure as mothers and fathers. But is it possible to treat your children equally? How should you respond when one of your children accuses you of playing favorites?

For stepparents, the problem becomes even more complex. Are you obligated to love or even to like your stepchildren as much as your own biological children? While some stepparents expect to have loving feelings quickly and automatically toward their stepchildren, that's unrealistic. Although there may occasionally be a honeymoon period between stepparents and stepchildren because they are exploring a new relationship, the shared history between parents and their biological children all but guarantees favoritism.

---

[3] Although it's obvious that growing up feeling undervalued in your family can lead to problems, it shouldn't be assumed that being the favored child is necessarily an advantage. Children who receive more parental attention than their brothers and sisters may worry about falling from grace if they make any mistakes. Some become highly anxious or feel guilty about how their siblings are being treated. Others develop an unhealthy sense of superiority. For that latter group, it can be quite a shock when they discover that they're not similarly revered by the rest of the world.

Perhaps the best way to handle this problem is to shift your focus completely away from treating siblings or stepsiblings equally. Instead, focus on fairness.

FAIRNESS

There are several things that you can do to avoid the problems associated with favoritism:

- Don't try to treat your children identically. As I mentioned earlier, this is an impossible and inappropriate task. Trying to do so only encourages them to keep score and to seek out petty differences that they can use in arguments with their siblings or with you. If you had ten children and made ten identical sandwiches, each of them would probably think that another got a better sandwich. The sandwiches (or other gifts) are irrelevant to their feelings about how they're viewed.

  Instead, emphasize fairness. Giving one child a skateboard and another a pair of roller skates, or sending one child to piano lessons and another to ballet class may be more fair and more rewarding than force-fitting both children into an activity only one of them likes.

- Look for ways to recognize and show respect for your children's differences. Doing so not only increases their self-esteem, it also avoids the problems and expectations that come with attempts at identical treatment. Remember that there's a difference between equity and equality. You can treat children fairly without treating them identically.

  Show them that just because you admire an older child's athletic or artistic abilities, the younger children don't have to do the same things to get your attention. Let them know about your pleasure, pride, and sense of wonder about their talents.

• Pay attention to your children's accusations of favoritism.
  Even if you think there is no basis for their complaints, it
  may be the only way they can express other frustrations.
  They may feel that it is safer to attack a parent, who
  probably will not reject them, than to express anger at
  someone who may, such as a coach.

  Instead of simply arguing the point, let them know
  that you can see they are upset. If the issue arose over
  making one child attend to a chore, like cleaning his
  room, keep the discussion focused on the task at hand. If
  the child's still upset later, return to the issue and talk
  about what's really bothering him. He's likely to find it
  easier to talk then, because you acknowledged his emotions earlier and because some time has passed so he
  could cool down.

• Try not to compare your children with one another. This
  often has the opposite effect from what parents intend,
  which is usually to motivate the unfavorably compared
  child. Think how resentful you would feel at work, for
  example, if someone asked you why you could not be like
  someone else.

  In families, this type of comment is even more damaging. Not only does the child who's unfavorably compared
  feel resentful, angry, and inadequate, but it also places a
  terrible burden on the apparently favored child.

• Hold family meetings. These can be good clearinghouses
  for gripes, including favoritism. Try not to be defensive if
  one of your children accuses you of giving preferential
  treatment to another. (In fact, the child's willingness to
  voice such a complaint is actually a backhanded compliment. It means your relationship is strong enough that he
  or she is willing to share sensitive and potentially damaging information with you.) Even if you feel the complaint
  is trivial or unfounded, acknowledge the intensity of your
  child's emotions as you discuss the problem.

Keep these family meetings informal. Serving popcorn or some other light snack can help set the tone. Allow everyone a chance to speak—although you may wish to set time limits or gently rein in complaints if they're not going anywhere beyond griping. (Some parents ask children to pair each complaint with a realistic and fair suggestion for correcting the situation.)

• Arrange for private time with each child. Although children may frame their concerns in terms of how much time you are spending with one of their siblings, the underlying issue often has more to do with the intensity of the attention than with the number of hours spent together.

If, for example, you're spending a lot of time helping a child with schoolwork or encouraging him or her on the sports field, don't feel you need to devote the same number of hours to each of the other children. Simply spending some regular time alone with a child who feels disfavored will go a long way toward that child feeling cared about. It can even be just fifteen minutes before bed, reading a book or playing with electric trains together.

GOOD RIVALRY, BAD RIVALRY

A friend of mine from graduate school, now a professor of psychology, described a scene he had recently witnessed. An eleven-year-old girl was taunting her eight-year-old sister as they climbed the stairs in a bookstore. "I hate you!" yelled the older girl. "I can't stand being with you! I just hate you!"

The younger girl was desperately trying to ignore her older sister's comments, but the strain showed on her face. Still, she wanted to be with her big sister, and was tagging along like a puppy. It was clear that this was not the first time they'd treated each other this way.

There are times when the bond between siblings appears tenuous at best. Brothers and sisters who seemed to get along fine a day or even an hour earlier will suddenly act like worst enemies. They cannot play together without yelling, hitting, or calling each other names. Psychologists and others who study sibling rivalry have found several clear patterns that can help parents anticipate and handle such battles.

According to research by Dr. Wyndol Furman of the University of Denver, the amount of conflict between children is not related to their affection for each other. In fact, he says, name-calling alone is seldom a reason for worry. Neither is a certain amount of pushing and shoving—although some siblings need to have limits set on their antics. ("No, you may not tie your sister to the tree!" or "No, you may not lock your brother in the basement!") If the sibling rivalry appears dangerous, cruel, or harmful, it's a good idea to get help from a child psychologist or psychiatrist to see if there are underlying medical or emotional problems. Parents should also become concerned if one or more of the siblings is also very aggressive toward other children outside the family.

Periods of apparent animosity between siblings seem to help children with their social development. Children can take more risks with a brother or sister because a sibling can't reject them the way friends might. In other words, from a child's point of view, if he wants to try out the latest verbal gibe or test the limits of acceptable behavior, he's much safer conducting those experiments on a sibling than on a parent, a teacher, or even a classmate.

Sibling fights apparently serve several other developmental and social functions as well. They are a way for children to learn and practice conflict-resolution skills that they'll need as they grow older. They allow children to establish that they are different from their brothers and sisters. (This is, perhaps, why the fights seem to be most intense when siblings are the same sex and very close in age.) They are a release for some of the anger and frustration children may be feeling toward an adult whom they would not dare treat the way they're treating a sibling.[4]

Another predictor of increased fighting between siblings is when one child enters a new social group that puts a premium on more adult behavior. For example, it's common for a child who's about to enter middle school or junior high school not to want to be associated with a younger sibling.

Fighting with a brother or sister can also be a way for children to try to determine the favored child in the family. Children who feel they are treated unfairly by their parents are more likely to fight with each other, according to Dr. Furman's research.

To adults, sibling squabbles can look and sound vicious and perhaps even dangerous. Such appearances are usually misleading. Pediatricians will tell you that they're much more likely to treat injuries from fights between children who aren't relatives than between siblings. A lot of the screaming is for the benefit of the parents and doesn't really reflect their real feelings about each other. The battles are, to borrow from Shakespeare (somewhat out of context), "full of sound and fury, signifying nothing."[5] When the parents are gone, the children often get along fine.

Intense rivalries that flourish during the early years often disappear or significantly diminish when children reach adolescence. The change reflects their growing sophistication in two areas. Their increased ability to empathize makes the older one, at least, less likely to try to bully someone smaller. Also, their growing cognitive skills help them learn the value of teaming up against their parents to get the things they want.

---

    [4] Sibling fights can be triggered by displaced anger toward a parent. It's a lot safer to be angry at your brother or sister than at your mother or father.
    [5] As long as I've dragged out that quote, I should tell you the other context in which I use a warped version of it. I have a fourteen-year-old cat named Zabar, who, in addition to being loving and sweet-tempered, is also what might be called intellectually challenged. In other words, he's wonderful but dumb. I refer to him as "A tail pulled by an idiot, full of sound (and furry), signifying nothing." He seems to like it.

RESPONDING TO RIVALRY

You should consider a number of factors when planning how to respond to battles between siblings:

- Remember that sibling rivalry is not only normal, but also adaptive. Let children settle their own arguments whenever possible. If you pay attention to the fighting, it tends to perpetuate the squabbles because they learn that fighting is an effective way for them to get you to drop whatever you're doing and rush over. If you don't intervene in their conflicts, in a couple of minutes the emotional storm will probably blow over and they'll be friends again.

- Use fights between your children as a way to encourage them to try new ways to solve their problems. Pay as much attention to their skills at arguing as you do to the things they're arguing about. Encourage them to empathize with the other person and to come up with several alternative solutions to their difficulties.

- When the noise level is too high, consider using the paradox of sibling rivalry to your advantage. It would seem that two people who say they hate each other would want to be apart. But this is seldom the case with fighting school-age siblings. Threatening to separate them if they cannot play quietly will often encourage them to cooperate.

- Remember that children will often mirror your emotions, even when you are unaware of how you feel. A sudden increase in the amount of fighting between siblings may be the children's way of coping with increased family tension.

- Try to identify the situations that trigger the rivalry. For example, some children fight with each other when they do household chores together. Others fight over who has the better job when they are assigned different tasks. Switching from solo to group chores, or vice versa, will sometimes eliminate the problem.

- When warring children come to you to settle a dispute, don't try to determine which child was at fault. There is no way you can figure out who hit whom first. Even if you could, assigning blame to one child will only perpetuate the battles.

    Tell them that if they can't play quietly together, they'll both have to go to their rooms. It's important to discipline them equally. If you punish only one, you'll escalate the sibling rivalry.

WHEN SIBLINGS ARE APART

A child psychiatrist friend of mine told me how, when he went off to summer camp when he was ten years old, it was the first time he and his eight-year-old sister had been separated. One evening the girl and her parents went to a restaurant. When the hostess asked how many people were in the party, the parents said three, but the girl insisted on correcting them by saying that they were really four, but that her brother was away for the summer.

Sometimes the bonds between siblings are more obvious when the children are apart than when they are together. The rivalry and squabbling that lead parents to wonder if their children will ever get along are frequently replaced by feelings of emptiness and depression. Often, brothers and sisters who are separated say they feel incomplete, and will search for symbolic reminders that the ties to siblings and family are still intact.

Parents sometimes underestimate the importance of the sibling relationship and what happens when that relationship is disrupted. The same parents who do a very good job of preparing a child for the addition of a new brother or sister may fail or forget to prepare that child for the temporary absence of a sibling.

Most children handle planned separations from siblings very well. After a few days, they learn to turn to their friends for emotional intimacy. In fact, some find that there are unforeseen benefits to being apart temporarily. A younger child may get extra attention. An older child may get to feel like an only child again. A quiet child who has been overshadowed may have an opportunity to blossom.

Some children have more trouble than others when apart from their brothers and sisters. Typically these are the children who made the most fuss when their parents first left them at child care or preschool. Or they may have recently suffered the loss of a grandparent or other close relative. Children whose parents are divorced or separated often find that being left by a sibling recalls earlier fears of abandonment.

Children of alcoholic, abusive, or otherwise dysfunctional parents often become extremely close as a way of surviving the added stresses of daily life. They usually find the thought of being kept apart very upsetting.[6]

Unexpected separations, as when a child is rushed to the hospital, are particularly stressful. Young children are often convinced that they are the underlying cause of the illness or accident. But they may keep those feelings to themselves. Parents may have to explain several times why the sibling entered the hospital, and repeatedly reassure the children that it was not their fault.[7]

---

[6] When you think about it, the underlying theme of the Hansel and Gretel fairy tale is that siblings can protect and rescue each other from dangerous and seemingly hopeless situations.

[7] This is true when children are traumatically separated from their parents as well. I wrote in an earlier book (*Parent & Child: Getting Through to Each Other* [New York: William Morrow & Company, 1991]) how I was convinced, when I was eight years old, that I had caused my father's death from colon cancer by having knocked the wind out of him when I'd hit him in the stomach with a baseball several years earlier. I was, of course, ashamed and frightened to admit my guilt to my mother. She figured it out, and relieved me of my guilt and fear.

The most subtle and confusing types of sibling separations occur when an older child, still at home, moves on to a new stage of development. For example, a twelve-year-old girl who routinely played with her ten-year-old sister may suddenly and dramatically move away both emotionally and in her interests. The older girl's new fascination with boys and social status may leave her younger sister feeling ignored and worthless. The younger child suddenly feels invisible.

That separation resolves itself as soon as the younger child moves into that next stage herself, or the older child feels secure enough in her new role to reconnect with the younger one. Meanwhile, the best thing you can do to help the younger sibling is to acknowledge that the apparent rejection hurts, and to let her know that things will get better.

MAKING SEPARATIONS MORE BEARABLE

Parents can ease the pain when siblings are separated. The approach taken depends upon the age of the child and the type of separation. Here are some things to keep in mind:

- If the separation is planned, encourage the child left behind to help the one who is leaving prepare for the trip. It is especially useful for a younger child to help an older one pack for camp, college, or even a planned stay in the hospital. That helps address the younger child's feelings of abandonment. It also helps correct any misconceptions the child may have about where the older sibling is going and whether she will be prepared.

- Expect the child who stays at home to want a symbolic representation of the sibling who left. This can be a photograph, or a toy belonging to the child who is gone. Occasionally, a young child may wish to sleep in the absent child's bed for a few days. All of these help a child feel connected to a sibling who is away.

- If the separation is traumatic, like a hospitalization, pay attention to the feelings of the children who remain home. Young children need to be reassured that they're not to blame for their sibling's problem. You may have to ask them directly if they think they are responsible. Even if they say no, it's a good idea to go over why their brother or sister is hospitalized, and how it had nothing to do with their thoughts or behavior.

- Encourage separated siblings to keep in touch. Young children may not think of writing or telephoning each other. They may not realize that they can visit. At the same time, don't force them to do so. Not all children will feel like it. What's important is that you offer them the opportunity.

   Another approach, if a child does not want to write a letter, is to suggest keeping a journal of her thoughts and activities while the other child is away. That way, when they're back together, they can talk about all that has happened.

WHEN A SIBLING'S DISABLED

The college-age daughter of a friend of mine once told me how, when she was growing up, she was jealous of the extra attention that her twin brother got from their parents. She was angry that she would be punished for misbehavior that he could get away with.

But she couldn't express those feelings directly to her parents. She was healthy; her brother was mentally retarded and had cerebral palsy and other neurological problems.

Only recently have health-care and child-development professionals looked closely at what it's like to be the sibling of a child who is emotionally, mentally, or physically disabled. They have found that the relationship is far more complex than they had anticipated, but that a few simple things can help both the children and their parents make the most of the situation.

Psychologists used to assume that having a child with a disability at home was damaging to other members of the family. Recent research has shown that while it adds to stress, it doesn't necessarily lead to damage. It can lead to creative problem solving and personal growth. Children who have disabled siblings can gain a greater appreciation of the value of different kinds of people and become more understanding of human differences.

To handle the stress successfully, children need increasing amounts of information about their disabled siblings and other family issues. This information has to be presented in ways that match their own developmental needs and abilities. A kindergartner, for example, may require reassurance that he didn't cause the sibling's problem, especially if the disabled child is younger. He may also need to know that he can't catch a disability the way he can catch a cold from a brother or sister.

Older school-age children often have to explain their sibling's disability to friends and classmates. They need to practice and master the social skills that will allow them to answer children's and adults' questions, even when they're unspoken. Adolescents, who are struggling with their own wishes for independence, need to know what the family's long-term plans are.

This may be the first generation in which people with disabilities are outliving their parents. Brothers and sisters sometimes feel that they will not be able to leave home or even go away to college because they may wrongfully assume that they'll spend the rest of their lives caring for the sibling who has special needs.

Having a disabled sibling can distort the natural rivalry between brothers and sisters. Competition for attention and individual recognition takes on a different tone, not only at home but at school.

Siblings of disabled children are often asked to assume responsibilities years before their classmates are. Some requests are made by their parents, like asking them to baby-sit for their brother or their sister every day after school. Other duties are self-imposed and based, in part, on how they view their roles within the family.

Many of these children feel a strong pressure to achieve. They need to be the scholar, the athlete, or the prom queen because they feel that their parents are disappointed by what their other child can't achieve. This added responsibility can breed resentment, at least temporarily. My friend's daughter remembered being upset at her parents because spending time with her brother after school meant that she could participate in only a few extracurricular activities. She felt they were taking away her rights as a child. As she grew older, however, she began to see that her parents were the ones who stayed with him during the weekend and got up with him in the middle of the night. She had only seen what *she* was giving up.

HELPING THE HEALTHY CHILD

A child who has an emotionally, mentally, or physically disabled brother or sister often feels isolated, especially in preadolescence, when fitting in with a peer group is of growing importance. Although social service agencies have long provided support groups for parents, only recently have such groups been available to siblings.

Unlike adult groups, children's groups tend to focus more on social activities than on talk. Sibling support groups help those children's self-esteem and give them a forum for sharing feelings that they may be uncomfortable telling their parents. They're well worth looking into.

Here are some other things parents should keep in mind:

- Arrange to spend time alone with each of your children. This is important for all families, but especially for those in which one child has some special needs. It guarantees some time, even if it's only five minutes a day, during which your children don't have to compete with each other for your attention and love.

  Also, talk to all your children about the perceived unfairness of the disabled child's getting more time and attention. This lets all your children know that you recognize and respect their needs.

• Acknowledge your children's feelings and fears, even if they're not directly expressed. Many children worry that there's something wrong with them if they're jealous or angry at their brother or sister. Let your children know that it's OK to have negative feelings toward the disabled sibling: Such thoughts don't make them bad kids, and you won't reject them because they have those feelings.

9

Sports and Games

Men trifle with their business and their politics; but never trifle with their games. It brings truth home to them. They cannot pretend that they have won when they have lost, nor that they made a magnificent drive when they foozled it.
—GEORGE BERNARD SHAW (1856–1950)

The six-year-old stood almost alone on his half of the soccer field. The ball had been deep in the other end of the playing field for several minutes, defying the young children's attempts to kick it either into the goal or back to the other half. The boy, who knew that the rules prohibited him from crossing the midfield line to the area with all the action, started feeling bored. A few moments later the coach, who was also the boy's father, looked in his son's direction and became angry.

"What are you doing there?" the coach yelled when he saw that the boy was upside down.

"I'm doing a headstand, Dad. Pretty good, isn't it?" came the boy's reply.

Jeffrey Vennell, the director of sports and recreation at the University of Rochester and the man who told me that story, uses it to teach parents and prospective coaches about one of the differences between the way young children and adults perceive sports. Many youth sports programs are overstructured and don't meet the needs of young children. What children need and want is to play.

Physical education researchers and sports psychologists have noticed a pattern in the way children of different ages approach participation in sports. Children in early grade school tend to enjoy sports for the sense of mastery they feel. Dribbling a ball and swimming from one end of the pool to the other are rewards in themselves. It doesn't matter that it takes them three tries or that they're doing it slowly. Children this age who play among themselves, as opposed to playing on local teams, show relatively little interest in competition.

Somewhere around puberty, which often occurs toward the end of elementary school, there's a change. Children begin to judge themselves as athletes on the basis of how well they do compared with someone else. Simply mastering the skills is no longer enough. Many children drop out.[1]

One generally accepted reason for this decline is that there is often too much emphasis placed on winning. This emphasis is a relatively new phenomenon among school-age children. In fact, there's been a significant shift over the past century in the types of games played by children.

Traditional children's games, such as tag, don't involve keeping score. Their rules are simple, and their style of play somewhat chaotic and exhausting. Over the past few decades these traditional games have been largely replaced by childlike versions of adult sports, such as shooting baskets or throwing a football. Specific sports skills have largely supplanted what used to be more general playing skills.

One of the strongest benefits of sports is that they give children an additional arena in which they can succeed. Success, however, is not the same as winning. It's the demonstration of competence.

---

[1] Studies by Dr. Glyn C. Roberts of the Institute of Child Behavior and Development at the University of Illinois at Urbana-Champaign have found that between the ages of twelve and sixteen, roughly 80 to 90 percent of children drop out of organized sports, especially competitive sports. He's found exactly the same pattern among adolescents who drop out of music, especially those who had participated in music competitions.

This seems to be particularly important for girls. For many years, the classroom was the only or main place girls could be successful. But the teacher-child interactions often made it more difficult for girls than for boys to feel competent.[2] By participating in sports, girls can get into a new environment where those problems aren't interfering.

EVALUATING A SPORTS PROGRAM

There are several things parents should pay close attention to when evaluating a sports program for children and deciding how active a role they wish to play in it:

- Find out how actively the child will participate in the sport, especially if the child is new to it or not very good at it. Surveys have found that the vast majority of young children would rather play on a losing team than sit on the bench of a winning team.

- Ask how much emphasis is placed on winning. Does that emphasis match your own beliefs? While some community baseball programs, for example, don't keep league standings or statistics such as batting averages, other communities publish those statistics in the local newspaper. The messages received by children in each situation about what is expected of them are dramatically different.

   Also, be sure to talk to your child about the differences between being successful and winning. Children often have difficulty differentiating between the two.

---

[2] For a fascinating look at how girls are still treated differently from boys in American schools—and the important consequences of such treatment—see *Failing at Fairness: How America's Schools Cheat Girls* by Drs. Myra and David Sadker (New York: Scribners, 1994).

- Don't push your child into a particular sport. The fact that you made the all-state football team may be an excellent reason for your child to want to play tennis.

- Don't become overinvolved in your children's sports. They may feel uncomfortable if you coach a team they're on, no matter how fair you are. They may be less willing to take risks when they know you might see them fail.

  Sports psychologists say that the type of involvement parents have in their children's sports is usually more important than the amount of involvement. The key is viewing the sport from the children's perspective and finding out how and if it's meeting their needs.

  For example, single parents who feel guilty that they can't attend all of their children's games may be perceived by the children as being very supportive and involved. It's a matter of attitude and interest as much as time.

COACHING YOUR CHILD

A man I interviewed a few years ago told me how his eleven-year-old son had signed up for a community basketball league. Another young player suggested that the boy's father become their coach. The father was eminently qualified—he'd coached a local university's team to an NCAA Division III championship that year! But after talking it over with his son, they both decided that it would be bad for their relationship.

That doesn't mean that all children whose fathers or mothers coach them on a team are doomed to failure. There are, however, special strains that go along with having a parent as a coach. Parents may feel uncomfortable seeing their child behaving just like any other kid. Children may feel that they're letting their parent down if they do something wrong on the field or court.

Community recreation programs for children, and even some

school athletics programs, depend upon parents to volunteer as coaches. Although coaches provide guidance, support, and discipline for their players, the coach-athlete relationship is very different from the parent-child relationship. Parents who understand the difference can minimize problems both on and off the playing field.

Part of the problem comes from the nature of children's sports programs. Organized athletics allow children to master a variety of both physical and social skills. As with any other attempts at mastery, children will struggle and fail a great deal of the time as they drop fly balls, miss foul shots, and lose their tempers. Having a parent as a coach makes those struggles and failures more public and potentially more embarrassing and frustrating. If children make mistakes on the ball field, they can leave them there with the coach when they go home after the game. If their parents are their coaches, the mistakes may come home with them and resurface as they are rehashed at dinner.

IF YOU WANT TO COACH OR WATCH

If you decide to become active in your children's athletics, either as a coach or as a fan, there are several things that you should bear in mind that will help prevent problems:

- Find out what your children think about your involvement. Some children, especially those who are under the age of ten or so, welcome their parents' participation. Others are much more reticent.

  Ask your child how she'll feel if you're coaching and she doesn't get to play. Ask her what would happen if the other players thought that by coaching your own kids you were playing favorites.

- Be sensitive to the values you foster by the way you talk about sports. Many young children take a much less competitive approach to sports than their parents or even their teenage siblings. They focus on mastering skills and having fun rather than keeping score.

Even so, the first question out of the mouths of a lot of parents when their children come home from a game is "Did you win?" That tells the child that you think winning is the most important thing, and hints that you'll be angry or upset if she did not.

Instead, ask your child, "Did you have a good time?" That changes the atmosphere completely, and helps the child cope more easily with competition.

- Try to separate your roles as coach and as parent. Remember that a great attribute of a sporting match is that you can leave it behind when it's over, and move on to something else. Rehashing a poorly played game at home will lead your children to resent you both as a coach and as a parent. Let your children control whether you talk about a game outside of practice.

- Before you begin, ask yourself why you're getting involved. Your stint as a coach has a much lower chance of success if your main goal is to build a winning team or to relive your own youthful exploits. Ask yourself how you and the children will know if you've been successful, even if you don't win many games.

Good Winners, Poor Losers

No child likes to lose. But there are some for whom not winning or not getting their way is a trigger for a tantrum or a pout. They'll storm off if their friends won't let them be the captain of the fantasy pirate ship. They'll knock over the checkerboard or walk away with the basketball if they're losing a game.

A certain amount of this behavior is normal and reflects a

child's stage of development. Toddlers and preschoolers, for example, don't yet have the words to express the intense emotions they feel. They're also experimenting with ways to handle their frustration and desire for control. They find it hard to lose for the same reason they find it hard to share toys with other children.

We expect to see a shift in this attitude by the time children are in elementary school. Unfortunately, that doesn't always occur. Research by Dr. Edward L. Deci, director of the Human Motivation Program at the University of Rochester, has found that older children and adults who are bad losers worry about what others think of them if they don't win, or feel that winning is what makes them good people.[3]

While the consequences of stomping off in a huff are minor when you're in kindergarten, such behavior can lead to more serious social problems among older children. Bad losers have more trouble than other children making and maintaining friendships. For some children the problem can become self-perpetuating, since their difficulty with friendships increases their feelings of worthlessness and, therefore, their need to win.

The reasons for becoming a bad loser rest in a combination of genetics and environment. Some children appear from birth to be easily frustrated and upset. Their temperaments make them more likely to become perturbed by situations that other children take in stride. More commonly, however, children who are bad losers are responding to the subtle messages they get from their families, teachers, and the mass media.[4]

---

[3] This, too, is a link to the typical thought processes of toddlers and young preschoolers. Children this age have a difficult time differentiating between *doing something* bad and *being someone* bad. That's one reason why any self-respecting three-year-old will deny raiding the cookie jar, even though there are crumbs and chocolate chip smears all over his face. He can't afford to admit he was a "bad" person, so he denies having done the "bad" thing.

[4] I find this to be particularly true during coverage of such events as the Olympics. Despite the number of "human interest" stories, and the repeated lip service paid to the efforts of the losing contestants, the real emphasis is placed on the winners. For example, the winner of the men's downhill ski race in the 1994 Olympics received worldwide acclaim. The fourth-place finisher was virtually ignored, even though he was only 26/100 of a second slower.

Children watch how their parents handle things when they're frustrated. They pay closer attention to what we do than to what we say when we're under stress. Some children who are sore losers have parents who are sore losers, who teach through their actions that getting angry is the way to handle frustration. The example set by parents may be subtle or blatant. Parents who never talk about their own disappointments or failures give their children an impossibly high standard to live up to. The implications of making mistakes or losing are blown out of proportion.

Even well-meaning questions like, "Did you do your best?" can unintentionally give some children a disturbing message. If they didn't do their best, they worry that their parents or coaches will view them as disappointments. If they did do their best and still failed, then perhaps they are hopeless.

Instead, it's a better idea to assume that whatever your child did, it was the best she could do on that particular day. Also, don't assume that a child's negative emotions in response to her performance are necessarily bad. That may not be true if those emotions are appropriate and in proportion.

Although all children have periods when they're short-tempered and have difficulty losing, it's seldom a sign of trouble if it occurs rarely and reflects the importance of the situation. We should expect children to be more upset if they lose the finals of a local basketball tournament, for example, than if they lose a spur-of-the-moment pick-up game. Children who treat those disappointments equally are probably seeing them as tests of their self-worth.

HELPING A SORE LOSER

Since children who are bad losers often have unrealistic expectations of themselves, one of the best things parents can do is to help them set goals that emphasize effort and improvement, as well as winning. Those goals might include passing the basketball well during the pressure of a game, or swimming two lengths of the pool nonstop.

Here are some other things you can focus on if you're concerned that your child finds it difficult to keep losing in perspective:

• Look at the subtle messages you're giving your child about failure. Many of these are unconscious and therefore very difficult to recognize. For example, if you have a big celebration when your child's team wins a game, but you just say, "Well, you tried," when they don't, you're teaching that you value winning much more than effort.

• Talk about some of your own frustrations with your children. Sore losers often worry that anything they don't succeed at will be shameful to their parents. This concern is compounded if they never see or hear about how family members handle disappointments. Don't feel you have to talk only about sports. Discuss how it felt when you didn't get the lead in the school play or when you got turned down for a job you really wanted.

• Let your children practice losing as well as winning. Young children take great glee in defeating their parents at simple card and board games. That gives them a sense of power that they relish. But consistently winning such games at home may set up unrealistic expectations for when they play with their friends.

   Don't let your children win all the time. Remember that they learn some important lessons from disappointment. Also, losing a game at home can be less threatening to children than losing one at a friend's house. It will make it easier for children to master the skills they need to recover emotionally and move on.

• Encourage your children to keep trying, even when they're frustrated. If bad losers don't feel they can be successful at an activity, they may not do it at all. Letting children know that you'll be proud of them simply for trying will often give them the incentive they need to re-double their efforts. If they persevere, they may find that they can master what they've been avoiding.

• Use television and newspaper coverage of sports to help children explore their own values. How would they feel if they fell during a skating competition or ski race? Why are the people who have no chance of winning competing?

Our children need help interpreting these issues, just as they need adult guidance interpreting the pictures of war that they see in the newspaper or on the evening newscast. If you're watching an event like the Olympics or a marathon race, point out people who are having fun or who are doing better than they had in the past.

• Encourage children to focus on the changes in their own performance and skills, not on the number of games they win. Focusing on performance and skills is, after all, what professional athletes and other successful people do.

RAISING A TALENTED ATHLETE

When I got off the phone after talking with a particular twelve-year-old girl, I was exhausted just thinking about her schedule. A typical Sunday during the winter included playing a basketball game and an indoor soccer game, and attending practice for yet another team she's on. In all, she's a member of three soccer teams and three basketball teams. Her parents have been encouraging her to explore her athletic talents, but are wary of pushing too hard. They said that if there comes a time when she wants to quit, they'll not stand in her way.

Sports can be a highly emotional area of children's relationships with their parents, especially for children who are athletically gifted. Parents who offer their child too little encouragement or support may leave her feeling that her talents are unappreciated. Those who become overly involved risk having their efforts backfire. If you push too hard, your children may feel that they're doing the sport for you instead of themselves. It gives them a target for their rebellion and a lever to use against you. They can punish you by not going out for a sport.

One of the biggest problems occurs when parents consciously or unconsciously use their children to make up for their own limited success in sports or other activities. Some parents see their child's performance as a reflection of their own success or failure. That's dangerous. Children quickly sense that their parents have more at stake in a football game or a gymnastics meet than they do.

The shift toward adolescents competing in the Olympics, and the growth in regional competitions for even younger competitors in many sports, has caused some parents to look for early signs that their children are athletically talented. While there are stories of children who could do fancy dribbles with a basketball in kindergarten or sink long putts at age six, experts in children's athletics say early signs can be misleading. Good coordination by itself does not lead to success in athletics. In fact, it's very difficult to tell at an early age whether a child will be an outstanding athlete.[5] Even if you could tell physically, you couldn't tell emotionally or psychologically.

HELPING A CHILD ATHLETE

While some children who feel pushed into athletic competition by their parents will address the issue by talking about it, others will show their discomfort without words. For example, children may develop recurring injuries as an ac-

---

[5] It works the other way, too. As Dr. Shane Murphy, a sports psychologist with the United States Olympic Committee, once told me, "We've had Olympians who, as very young children, were seen as klutzes."

ceptable way of getting out of a sport when they feel too much pressure. Those injuries are real, not faked, although the child may use them as a way of saving face in front of her parents.

Here are some questions to ask to help decide if you're providing enough support or making too many demands on a child athlete:

- Is your child soliciting your opinion? This is more important than whether your child actually follows your advice. Children who feel pressured by their parents often try to avoid talking to them about the sport. If your child is asking for your input, that's a sign that you're doing it right. If your child appears withdrawn, moody, or distant, that's a sign of possible trouble.

- Are you taking responsibility for your child's schedule? A child who enjoys a sport will usually want to handle some of the administrative work that goes with it, like writing a practice schedule on a calendar. If you try to give more responsibility to your child and she doesn't take it, that's a sign that she's feeling pushed too hard.

- Are you forcing your child to compete at higher levels? Children who are enjoying a sport will seek competition that challenges them. Forcing them to compete at inappropriately high levels will only frustrate and discourage them, since they know they cannot be successful.

  Moving a child to the next level is right when the child is enjoying competition and making progress. It's wrong when you're pushing to "improve" or "toughen up" your child.

- Are you imposing your own emotional agenda on your child? Remember that left to themselves, children will derive much more pleasure from seeing their own improvement in a sport than from the final score of a game or their standing in a tournament. They also like to sample a variety of sports instead of homing in on one. If you're feeling lots of disappointment because your child wants to try something else, that's a clear sign that you've been over-involved.

IF YOUR KID'S A KLUTZ

Despite the comment by the U.S. Olympic Committee's sports psychologist in the footnote on page 181, for some children it's obvious, even by the time they're in kindergarten, that they'll never play tennis on the center court at Wimbledon or take the field at Yankee Stadium. Child development professionals describe these children as having difficulties with gross and fine motor skills. But on the playground, their classmates simply refer to them as klutzes.

Being a klutz has increasingly profound social and even academic implications as a child passes through elementary school and into adolescence. It interferes with social relationships and often decreases preadolescents' self-esteem, especially among boys.

Psychologists and early physical education teachers are paying much more attention these days to the social and academic problems that often go along with clumsiness. They're also developing ways to help these children improve in areas that may, at first glance, appear unrelated.

For example, children with poor physical coordination may have trouble focusing their attention on academic tasks at school as well. Basic concepts, like "over," "under," and "through," are often more difficult for them to understand. Researchers have found that clumsy children are at a greater risk for significant social problems starting as early as the first grade. Motor skills form a big part of young children's self-concepts and how they perceive others. Children who have problems with coordination tend not to have as many friends who will play with them.

Young children develop physical skills at different rates and times. In general, being a few weeks or even a few months late mastering one or two basic feats of coordination, such as sitting up, walking, or running, does not have any long-term consequences. But you should pay closer attention if there is a broader and consistent pattern of delays and difficulties. About 5 percent of children have noticeable trouble with coordination. In many cases, the problems don't go away by themselves. Studies have shown that about 50 percent of the children who have these problems at around age five still have them at age nine.

Most of the children seeking help to overcome clumsiness are boys. But it's unclear whether this is so because they have more problems with coordination or because their parents and teachers have higher expectations for them.

There's recent evidence that many of the children whom parents and teachers describe as uncoordinated have underlying problems with their sense of balance. Some may have to consciously work at sitting upright—the things that other children do automatically by the time they're toddlers. If you put these children in a classroom where they have to sit in a chair and write a report, much of their energy is concentrated on simply sitting. They can't pay as much attention to the more advanced task. Providing these children with some extra physical support in their chairs will often improve their school performance.

HELPING BUILD COORDINATION

Improving a child's physical coordination takes practice. While most children find physical activity fun, those who are clumsy often see sports and games as yet another opportunity to fail or to be rejected.

Here are some things you can do to help:

- Play active games with your child. Some of the children whose parents don't play catch with them and chase them around as toddlers and preschoolers have trouble keeping up physically with their peers by early elementary school.

Remember that, during the early years, it's more important that your child have fun throwing a ball than that he do it well. If your child is laughing, you're both doing a good job.

- Work on skills that require balance. Balance is fundamental to coordination. Pretend with your child that you're circus performers as you walk along a line on the sidewalk or on a narrow board. Try roller-skating or ice-skating. Again, begin by focusing on enjoyment more than technique.

- Work on both fine and gross motor skills. The two don't always go together. Some children are highly skilled at using their fingers for delicate tasks like handwriting or threading beads, but they may be poor at gross motor skills like jumping or running.

- Show some sympathy. If your child says he's no good at sports and has trouble hitting a ball, let him know that you know how upsetting that can be. If you argue or say it isn't important, your child is less likely to listen.

  A good next step is to help your child realize that he is not a total failure. This can be done by focusing on an activity in which he is more successful. For example, a child who says he's no good at baseball may actually be quite good at catching a ball. But he may be so distracted by his hitting problems that he only pays attention to that aspect of the sport.

- Enroll your child in an after-school sports program. Unfortunately, some of these programs may make a clumsy child feel even worse. One sign of a good program for young children is that it emphasizes personal accomplishments rather than winning. There should be lots of one-on-one coaching and encouragement. Also, if all the program offers are team sports, your child may become even less enthusiastic and self-confident.

Interview the people who run the program. Watch several sessions, and talk with other parents who have children in the program. Remember that young children are much more interested in having fun and improving their skills than in winning.

• Provide a safe environment for your child to build skills. Some one-on-one coaching, either by you, a coach, a teacher, or an older child, can help an awkward child catch up with his peers. So will some informal family games that allow you not only to give some discreet pointers, but also to praise progress. Expect your child to test how you will react to failure. Will you get angry or give up?

Don't overdo this practice. Twenty minutes a day is usually much more effective than three hours a day.

• Don't let your child become inactive. Children who feel that they cannot keep up with their peers or perform well enough may respond in ways that make the problem worse. They may avoid all athletic games and become sedentary. You may have to do some unpopular things, such as unplugging the television, to encourage your child to play.

IO

Social Development

> *We have not passed that subtle line between childhood and*
> *adulthood until we move from the passive voice to the ac-*
> *tive voice—that is, until we have stopped saying, "It got*
> *lost," and say, "I lost it."*
> —SYDNEY J. HARRIS (b. 1917)

The grade-school years are a time of tremendous emotional and social growth. Even the youngest grade-school children behave very differently from toddlers. And we expect such differences. Still, although they are socially more sophisticated, they view the world through a different lens than adults or even adolescents. Adults often have trouble seeing things from their children's perspective, and may misinterpret their behaviors. A classic example of this is certain behaviors that adults interpret as rudeness.

A child psychiatrist told me of a six-year-old boy who was referred to him by a teacher for a "behavior problem" that gravely concerned her. Here's how the psychiatrist pieced together the real story:

The boy loved watching professional football on television. He noticed that when players like something a teammate has done, they sometimes quickly pat him on the rump. So when his first-grade teacher did something that the boy really appreciated, he acknowledged it by casually walking over and patting her. She panicked and immediately referred him to the shrink.

What the teacher interpreted as rudeness or worse, the boy had intended as a compliment.[1] Rude behavior is a universal part of childhood. Yet many of the things that parents and teachers classify as obnoxious or provocative are quite different from one another and serve different purposes. So can the same behavior in different situations.

A child who insults or sticks out his tongue at another child is probably sending a different message than the one who insults or sticks out his tongue at a parent or teacher. When rudeness is directed at another child, it is often like teasing; it helps children define who is in a particular social group. Members of that group share their own patterns of teasing and rudeness toward each other. An outsider who tries to do the same things is rejected. The rude behavior helps the children in the group form bonds with one another, precisely because what they are doing cannot be done with others.

When the rudeness is directed at an adult, it is often to gain attention or to test the limits of acceptable behavior and the consequences of breaking the rules. But rude behavior may also be innocent, especially if the child is behaving that way for the first time. He may simply be mimicking behavior that gained attention somewhere else. The laugh tracks of television programs are often loudest after children or adults behave rudely toward each other.

Equally important in misinterpreting rudeness is a mismatch between parental expectations for their children's behaviors, and the behaviors that are truly appropriate for children that age.[2] In

---

[1] This sometimes becomes an issue for children whose ethnic or home culture is different from the dominant culture of their school. For example, some children are taught at home that it is rude to look an adult who's in authority, such as a teacher, directly in the face. They are taught that they should look at the floor when addressing the teacher as a sign of respect. But the teacher may interpret the child's cast-down eyes as a sign of evasiveness or even rudeness.

[2] A child psychiatrist acquaintance of mine told me a wonderful example of this that involved his own son, then three years old. The family lived in Seattle, and the boy was used to donning the requisite rainwear before heading off to preschool in the morning. Over the Christmas holiday, the psychiatrist and his wife took their son with them to Hawaii for a vacation. Instead of being thrilled (which was the

fact, the abstract concept of rudeness is confusing to many young children. There is nothing inherently wrong with nose picking in public or sticking out one's tongue. But suppressing such actions requires that children learn a system of adult rules that to them appear illogical and arbitrary.

RESPONDING TO RUDENESS

There are several things you should keep in mind if you feel that your children are behaving rudely:

- Avoid overreacting. Parents often find their child's rude behavior particularly upsetting because they are worried either about what other adults will think of them as parents, or about whether there is something fundamentally wrong with their child. Remember that occasional rude behavior is, by itself, seldom a cause for concern. It's much more important to look at whether your child is making friends and doing well in school.

  If, however, the child's rude and inappropriate behavior is getting him into trouble at school, or if the child acts rudely at home all the time, it's a good idea to seek professional help. The repeated rudeness may be a cry for help in handling other issues which the child does not know how to express more directly.

- Know your child's limitations. It's tempting, especially with bright children, to assume that they know and understand more than they do. For example, a kindergartner may not truly understand what you mean when you say a particular behavior is rude. If she sticks out her tongue at

---

parents' expectation), the boy was upset at the disruption to his schedule. When they arrived in Hawaii, he refused to take off his galoshes. In fact, he insisted on wearing them with his swimsuit to the beach. His behavior was neither rude nor defiant. It was a sign that the rainwear meant different things (e.g., security, predictability) to the boy than to the parents.

someone, explain that it's rude because it might hurt that person's feelings.

• Be careful how you respond to your child's rudeness. It's self-defeating to embarrass your child because she has embarrassed someone else, or to hit her as you tell her not to hit another child. By doing so you will teach your child that rude behavior is something that adults can do.

   Instead, state the rule and the reasons behind it in simple terms. ("You don't make that noise because it might hurt the other person's feelings.") Then give the consequences of breaking the rule. ("If you make that noise again, you will have to spend five minutes in your time-out chair.")

• Remember that your own rudeness and your laughter at rude behavior give children a confusing message. Children thrive on any form of attention they get from their parents. They learn what is acceptable by watching the important adults in their lives and mimicking them. Parents sometimes inadvertently perpetuate rude behavior in their children by paying attention to it, laughing at it, or even doing it themselves.

• Suggest alternative behavior to your child. Although it seems obvious to adults, a young child who is told not to talk when his mouth is full of food may not realize that if he swallows the food it will be all right to talk. Or if your child jumps up and down on the seat in a restaurant, suggest something more appropriate that she can do while sitting quietly.

TATTLING

In many homes—especially those with two or more children—children vie for the parents' attention with what sound like regular reports from the battlefield. "He kicked me!" "She took my ball!" "But he started it!" Each vivid description is a request for attention crafted with its own spin on the facts. The goal of each side is justice, revenge, and vindication. No matter how the parents respond, the goal remains elusive and the battle rages on.

Although tattling is universal among children, it has different meanings at different ages. Toddlers and preschoolers may sound like they are tattling when they are simply giving their parents uncensored information. Children this young joyfully share the things they have observed, but seldom make judgments about the people involved. They just want their parents to know what is going on in their world.

With school-age children, however, talking about someone else's behavior can take a different and more manipulative tone. There is much more to tattling than issuing a simple news report. To children this age, tattling is a power play. Although the focus of the tattle may be a problem, it's not an attempt to solve it. Instead, it's a way for a child to try to look good by making someone else look bad.

The most common targets are brothers and sisters, for tattling is a tool of sibling rivalry. It's a way for a child to position himself as an ally of his parents, worthy of extra love and attention. Even when the ploy is successful, the benefits quickly disappear. Siblings soon catch on to what has happened and respond by tattling on the tattler. It's a battle that neither side can win, but that no one will voluntarily stop, for fear of being the only loser.

Often the best way to handle the situation is to refer it back to the children. Don't make your children's problems—at least the ones that usually lead to tattling—your own. Instead, help them develop the tools they need to solve the issues they're complaining about. Such resolutions are often best worked out away from parents anyway. Having the children working out their problems by themselves will help them feel more self-reliant.[3]

But some children don't have the means to solve those problems. For them, tattling is a symptom of underlying difficulties with normal social skills. They are unable to settle the day-to-day conflicts in their lives in ways that are appropriate for their age. For example, they do not think about negotiating when another child wants one thing and they want something else. They rely on adults as their first line of defense instead of a last resort.

Among their peers, these children tend to be unpopular, neglected, or rejected. Persistent tattlers need help recognizing what it is they are doing wrong. They also benefit from supervised practice and coaching in ways of solving social problems by themselves. Although parents often provide such coaching, there are also a growing number of school-based programs on how to make and keep friends.

Other children have trouble telling the difference between tattling and sharing appropriate information with an adult, as when another child is in danger. They may be reluctant to ask for outside help, even when it is needed. In those situations, it's a good idea for parents to tell their children that in this family, we take care of each other. Saying that someone in the family needs help isn't tattling.

RESPONDING TO TATTLING

If you're concerned that your child is a tattletale, here are some things that can help:

---

[3] As with many matters that involve sibling rivalry, there's a seeming paradox that you can put to use. If your children are becoming loud or destructive, separate them by sending them to different rooms for a few minutes. As an adult, you would think that this type of separation is exactly what squabbling children would want. Instead, they view it as a punishment.

- Label the behavior. Tell the child that he is tattling and that you don't like it. Explain that he has nothing to gain from tattling. Make sure your child knows the difference between tattling and reporting important information, as when another child is in trouble or might be hurt.

  This is especially important for preadolescents, who feel a tremendous amount of social pressure not to talk about how their friends may be riding on bus bumpers, abusing drugs, or doing something else that is dangerous. Let your children know that they can come to you if they're really scared. They should learn to trust their feelings about that.

- Once you are sure your child knows what tattling is, try not to pay attention to it whenever it occurs. Keep in mind, however, that there's an important difference between ignoring the tattling and ignoring the child. Let your child know that you understand her feelings by saying, for example, that you can see how angry or sad she is. Then ask her how she might be able to solve that problem by herself. What other things might she do that don't involve you?

  Children who do the most tattling may not have tried any other way to solve their interpersonal problems. If, for example, a girl's young brother is pinching her, you could teach her to try a series of escalating responses, starting with simply telling him to stop.

- Don't punish a child whose behavior you have not seen. That gives the tattler too much power and, in the long run, works against you. If you punish the child who's being tattled on, you're strongly encouraging the tattler to keep doing it. You're also letting the punished child know that tattling on the first child is a good way of seeking revenge. Both of those things will cause more problems than they solve.

Heroes and Hero Worship

A developmental psychologist friend of mine confided that when he was in elementary school he wanted to be like his favorite cartoon character, Mighty Mouse. As an adult, he understood the psychology behind his choice. Mighty Mouse was physically small, but so powerful and quick-witted that he could solve the problems of the world.

Selecting heroes is a hallmark of childhood and preadolescence. It's a way of trying out new roles and coming to terms with both powerlessness and power. The choice of a hero reflects not only the child's stage of social development, but also her relationship with her parents and her perceptions of herself.

Most toddlers and preschoolers see their parents as heroes. In the eyes of children of that age, their parents seem to know everything and can do anything. For those few years, children see their parents as perfect, godlike beings.

During early elementary school, children realize that their parents have flaws, and they may search for a hero who's an idealized parent. The popular athlete becomes a fantasy father; the famous actress is imagined as their mother. It's not so much that the young child wants to be like these people as that she wants to be cared for by them. These fantasies allow children a safe way of struggling with the ambivalent but strong feelings they have toward their parents.

Children's early heroes from outside the family are often fictional characters. By following those characters' adventures, children can explore new ways of interpreting and handling the situations they face in their own lives. In fact, they are likely to adopt the behaviors and values of the people or fictional characters they look up to and identify with.

Choosing a cartoon character as a hero is quite common among children in kindergarten and early elementary school. It's a child's view of what a strong adult is (or, at least, should be like). That's why even a young child will usually admit that he doesn't really expect to be flying through the air like his hero Superman.

Many of these cartoon characters—especially those selected by boys—are quite violent. Their selection reflects the natural feelings of anger with which preschoolers and children in early elementary school are struggling to come to terms. The hero can act out in ways that the child dares not, and identifying with this character may allow the child a safe and vicarious way of expressing his strong emotions.

The heroes of older children are more likely to be real people, or at least human characters from books, television, or the movies. One reason for this shift in the type of hero children find attractive is that the hero serves different developmental purposes to older children. By identifying with a larger-than-life character, a child can sample how it feels to be brave or romantic, famous or attractive. Heroes offer a youngster a chance to sample adolescence while he's still a child, and adulthood while he's still a young teenager.

Children often use television to search for heroes. In addition to emulating their behavior, children use these television heroes as common ground for talking to each other.[4] From as early as they can control the channel being watched, however, boys and girls tend to select different programming. Boys generally choose programs with strong male characters, and girls tend to choose programs with strong female characters.

Unfortunately, that makes the hero-selecting task much more difficult for girls, since the majority of heroic characters on television and in the movies are male. Usually girls looking for a heroine to emulate must look much harder and must choose from among a smaller variety, at least on television and in film.

The implications of this gender gap may go well beyond childhood fantasies. Boys see men in just about every job imaginable. Girls may feel more limited because they don't see women doing

---

[4] Don't be surprised if your child—especially one in early elementary school—has a great deal of difficulty differentiating between a character in a film or television program and the actor who plays him.

the same things. They may not envision themselves in a particular career or adult role simply because they've never seen a woman—even an actress—in that role.

HELPING YOUR CHILD CHOOSE A HERO

Parents can play an active role in helping their children select and make the most of the heroes they emulate. Here are some suggestions:

- Read and tell stories to your children. Greek mythology and the Bible are filled with stories of the heroes of their time. So are African and Chinese folk tales. Start with short stories and fables to see what your child likes.

  When you read a story about a person from years ago, help your child reframe it from a modern perspective. (Was Ferdinand Magellan the sixteenth-century equivalent of an astronaut?) That makes the characters more real and alive than just a comic book or a cartoon.

- Talk about your own childhood heroes and why you admired them. Children seldom think of their parents as anything other than adults. By sharing stories and feelings from your own childhood, you offer your children new perspectives on what you're like as a person as well as a parent.

  Use this conversation as a springboard to let your children tell you what they like best about their heroes. It will probably be the first time they've thought seriously about it and put those feelings into words. If their heroes are fictional, help them think of real people who have some of the same characteristics.

- Help your child distinguish between a hero's goals and actions. Many of the fictional characters admired by children use very violent means to achieve their noble goals. Talk to your children about other ways those characters might have approached the problems they faced.

If you're concerned by your child's choice of a hero, don't just try to deny or downgrade it. Instead, build on your child's choice by introducing her to stories about similarly heroic people and characters who have different and more appropriate values.

PEER PRESSURE

One of the most difficult tasks of childhood is to learn how to resist social pressure. The challenges come from many directions: a dare to shoplift a pack of baseball cards, an invitation to use an illegal drug, a demand for sexual intimacy, an offer to join a gang.

Resisting such pressure is more complex than it appears. It requires that children think about the possible consequences of their behavior and that they feel strong enough to risk rejection. It also requires a sense of empathy for the person applying the pressure, and the ability and self-confidence to propose different and more appropriate behaviors.[5]

It's clear that children need to learn refusal skills just as they need to learn such basic living skills as tying their shoes. But programs that teach refusal skills must recognize that children view these situations differently than adults do. For example, while adults may focus on the long-term health consequences of smoking cigarettes, children tend to focus on the short-term benefits. A preteenage girl may so strongly believe that smoking will help her stay thin that she will pay little attention to warnings about a higher

---

[5] That's why simplistic solutions, such as the Reagan-era motto "Just say no!" are doomed to failure. They may sound good politically, but they don't take into account the social and developmental issues children are facing when they make such decisions. In fact, I used to have a sign in my office that read " 'Just say no!' has done for drug abusers what 'Have a nice day!' has done for chronic depressives."

risk of cancer. But she may be much more concerned by the fact that smoking will give her bad breath and increase the wrinkles in her face, two issues which affect her immediate goal of physical attractiveness.

Researchers who have studied how children respond to social pressures of all types have found that some are more likely than others to cave in. At particular risk are those children who feel few emotional ties to their families. If a child is lonely and isolated, and a group comes along that offers membership and a sense of affiliation, the child may welcome that, even if the group is a gang or a bunch of drug abusers.

A child whose parents are domineering is also at risk for being manipulated, even though the parents often think such an upbringing inoculates their child. A child who does only what he's told by his parents is prepared to listen to and not to question other authority figures. If, however, he has practice making his own decisions, then he's prepared to make his own decisions when it really counts. Moreover, children who have experience making choices that are not crucial feel more confident with more difficult decisions as they mature.

Learning how to respond to social pressure is a skill that is separate from moral values and personal philosophies. Like other skills, it's sharpened more through coaching and practice than by dogma. Telling a child simply to refuse or explaining the logical reasons why a child shouldn't do something doesn't go far enough. Such simple-minded approaches ignore the very real social pressures felt by children, and don't give them skills in maintaining relationships while refusing to give in.

A child who can respond to a friend's invitation to get drunk with a simple counteroffer to go to a movie is more likely not only to avoid problems with alcohol, but also to maintain the friendship. Simply saying no is seldom enough to get a child out of a situation, especially if that child's being pressured by a friend or someone she would like to become a friend.

BUILDING APPROPRIATE RESISTANCE

Here are some things you can do to help your children learn to resist unhealthy or inappropriate peer pressure:

- Talk about the decisions—both good and bad—you make as an adult and the ones you made as a child. Think through some of those decisions out loud, evaluating the short-term and long-term pros and cons. Help your child see how you weighed the alternatives. Try to weave these discussions in and out of your daily conversations with your children instead of making them formal, sit-down talks.

- Give children practice making decisions. With young children, this can be as simple as choosing which cereal to eat for breakfast, what clothes to wear to school, and which baseball cards to trade. The process of making a decision and being responsible for its outcome is much more important than the choice itself.

  Talk to your children about how they make specific, ordinary decisions. Help them explore the reasons behind such choices as whether they want to play with a particular classmate ("She plays fairly. I feel good about myself when I'm with her. She has nice toys and is willing to share them") or whether to try a new food ("It looks yucky. I've never tried anything that color before"). Use this as a way of helping your child get better at thinking through alternatives.

- Do some role-playing with a group of children and perhaps their parents. Act out some skits with your children that involve real-life situations in which they have to make a choice. What should you do if someone dares you to ride on the back bumper of a bus? What if you haven't finished your homework and someone you really like asks you to go to the movies? What if someone offers you a cigarette, a drink, or some drugs at a party? Does it matter if that person's a stranger or a good friend?

Have the children try solving these problems in different ways to see what the responses might be. Then they can talk about whether their responses sound phony or effective.

- Expect your child to make some bad decisions. Mistakes do not mean that you or your child has failed.[6] Remember that it's better for your child to make some mistakes—and to learn how to recover from them—when the stakes are relatively small than when she's an adolescent or adult and may suffer more serious consequences.

THE MOVE TO ADOLESCENCE

The end of elementary school is a watershed in a child's development. Several social and biological events take place in rapid succession.[7] Schools are larger and structured differently, with

---

[6] That's another problem with the "Just say no!" type of approach. It implies that someone who says yes, even once, is a bad person. But most of the children who say yes once or twice to alcohol or drugs don't go on to have major problems. It can be normal experimentation.

If you discover that your child has tried alcohol once or twice, for example, try not to panic or to respond dramatically. (Also, don't believe that you can "control" your child's behavior at this age. The more you try to control him, the more he'll look for ways to prove that you can't.)

Instead, talk about your concerns about the consequences of drinking alcohol, especially at his age. Remember that children are much more concerned with the present and the immediate future than any long-term risks. The thought of vomiting in front of his friends at a party is likely to be a more powerful argument against drinking than the possibility of liver damage.

Also, make your stance clear. If you don't think he should be drinking alcohol at all, say so. Ask him about the pressures he felt to drink. Talk about and practice alternative ways of responding when someone offers him alcohol.

[7] While little can be done about the biological issues, educators have begun helping students with some of the social issues by restructuring schools. Growing numbers of students in the United States are attending middle schools (approximately grades five through eight) instead of traditional junior high schools. There's

children moving to different rooms every hour or so. Their bodies are changing as they pass through puberty. And they are thinking differently, dealing with more abstract concepts, and relishing the ability to see gradations of gray in arguments instead of simply black and white.

These are topics worthy of an entire book rather than a section of a chapter. (In fact, that is what the fourth and final book in this series will be about.) Yet some of the critical issues of adolescence—exploring autonomy and independence, forming a separate identity, testing limits—may seem strangely familiar. Parents and children have tasted them before during the toddler years. (That's why I sometimes tell the parents of a two-year-old not to think of their child as a big baby, but as a short teenager.)

Many parents feel a sense of concern or even dread at the thought of their children passing through adolescence. This, too, is similar to toddlerhood, with its sobriquet "The Terrible Twos." Yet researchers say that much of the concern about dramatic and destructive shifts in teenage behavior is overblown. While adolescence in general and pubertal development in particular may lead to new types of behavior, a child's basic approach to life will remain the same. Happy children will tend to stay generally happy. Adventuresome children will seek new ways of achieving the excitement they crave. Children who have strong moral values will tend to maintain them.

Still, this is a good time to pause and reflect not only on what is to come, but on the remarkable things your child has accomplished. The incremental changes are so small that they usually slip by us unnoticed, only to appear as dramatic flashes of insight and memories. ("Gee, that twelve-year-old was once a baby inside of me!" "I remember when you were in diapers and were struggling to sit up. Now you want to baby-sit for someone else's child.")

It's also a good time to think about how you have changed as

---

also a recognition that many preteens and teens feel emotionally lost and ignored in the larger schools they attend, so educators are developing "schools within a school," a set of smaller groups of students who share certain classes and advisers so that a group of teachers get to know them reasonably well.

a parent. What were the issues, such as toilet training, that seemed so overwhelming at the time, but now appear trivial or are long-forgotten? Do you have trouble remembering what it was like not to have children? (I vaguely recall seeing a lot more movies in theaters instead of on videotape, and being able to go to a restaurant on the spur of the moment.)

And so I'd like to propose that you think of adolescence as a period that describes changes and growth not only for your child but for yourself. You are both headed toward a new set of challenges, frustrations, and satisfactions.

In previous books I've talked about the need to maintain a sense of humor as a parent. Our task is far too serious to be taken seriously all the time. It is the ability to laugh at ourselves that will get us through the inevitable rough spots of adolescence and beyond. Good luck, and have fun together.

Index

school (*continued*)
  change of, 8–13, 63
  cheating in, 39–41, 129
  counselors, 13, 52, 142
  dropping out of, 23
  fear of, 19
  grades, 24–27
  and home connection, 46–67
  midyear transfers of, 11–12
  parental involvement in, 46–57
  parent-teacher conferences, 26,
    26*n*, 45, 48–49, 51
  parent-teacher disagreements at,
    49–53
  preparation for, 4–8
  programs after, 146
  repeating grade vs. promotion in,
    13–18, 44
  "social promotion" in, 14, 14*n*
  sports programs after, 185
  summer, 36
  summer activities of, 11
  transitional kindergartens and first
    grades, 17
  transition to, 1–18
  when to begin, 13
Schulz, Charles, 152
secrets, 92, 96–99
self-concept, 41
self-control, 148
self-deception, 135
self-discipline, 148
self-esteem, 112, 130, 133, 144, 150,
  158, 169, 183
self-image, 54, 130
self-protection, 135
self-reliance, 85, 192
sense of humor, 150, 202
separation, 2, 4–5, 78*n*, 83–84, 126
Sesame Street, 2
sex differences, 92
sexual activity, 143
Shakespeare, William, 162
Shaw, George Bernard, 86, 171
shoplifting, 137, 138, 140
siblings, 152–170
  of disabled children, 167–170
  in dysfunctional family, 165
  fair treatment of, 158–160
  favoritism with, 155–160

privacy of, 95
rivalry of, 155–156, 160–164, 168,
  191, 192*n*
separation of, 164–167
stepparents and, 157
temperamental differences in, 153–
  155
Silver, Larry B., 21
single-parent families, 4*n*, 47, 97, 174
Sloan-Kettering Cancer Center, 78
smoking, 82*n*
social development, 2, 187–202
social problems, 37, 43, 149
"social promotion," 14, 14*n*
social skills, 13, 16–17, 145, 148,
  168, 175, 192
South Carolina, University of, 11
Southern California, University of, 82
spanking, 107–108, 147
spoiling children, 121–124
sports, 148, 171–186
  after-school programs of, 185
  children talented in, 42, 180–183
  coaching children in, 174–176,
    185, 186
  evaluating programs of, 173–174
  for girls, 173
  uncoordinated children and, 183–
    186
stealing, 129, 131, 137–140
stepfamilies, 89–91
stress, 7, 11, 36, 77, 121, 147, 168,
  178
  coping with, 68–85
study habits, 23, 41, 63
summer school, 36
superstition, 4
surrogates, 4, 181

tantrums, 61, 69*n*, 176
tattling, 191–193
teacher-parent conferences, 26, 26*n*,
  45, 48–49, 51
teacher-parent disagreements, 49–53
television, 30, 36, 71, 74–75, 75*n*,
  101, 122, 144, 177, 180, 188,
  195, 195*n*
Terence, 106
Thurber, James, 28
time out, 106